PENGUIN HANDBOOK
PH115

Play and Playthings for the Preschool Child

Elizabeth Matterson was born in 1930. She trained as a domestic science teacher at Leicester Domestic Science College, and taught cookery, housecraft, and needlework for several years. She first became interested in playgroups and play material when her youngest son was unable to get into a nursery school. She played an active part in founding a cooperative playgroup in Abingdon, and is now Chairman of the National Association of Pre-School Playgroups and President of the Berkshire branch of this association. She works as a Course Tutor to nursery nurses in training at the Oxford College of Further Education, and is interested in all aspects of child welfare and education.

Elizabeth Matterson is married to a scientist working at Harwell, and has two young sons.

PLAY
and
PLAYTHINGS
for the
PRESCHOOL
CHILD

by
E. M. MATTERSON

EDITED WITH A FOREWORD BY
EVELYN BEYER

PENGUIN BOOKS
BALTIMORE · MARYLAND

Penguin Books Inc, 3300 Clipper Mill Road, Baltimore, Maryland 21211

First published in England by Penguin Books Ltd, 1965, under the title
PLAY WITH A PURPOSE FOR UNDER-SEVENS

This revised edition published 1967

Printed in the United States of America

Contents

v

Foreword

Mrs. MATTERSON has written a practical little book in support of the thesis that play is an important concern of early childhood and, as such, deserves the attention and thoughtful action of parents as well as teachers of preschool children.

This is not a new thought, but it is one that is receiving extra attention from educators today, in the effort to provide meaningful play experiences for "culturally deprived" groups of children when preparing them for a more satisfying and successful school experience.

Susan Isaacs, British educator and psychoanalyst, in her volumes describing intellectual and social growth of children, found her richest material in observations of children's unstructured play situations. She observed that play leads to discovery, reasoning, and thought, that play is a bridge to social relations, and that play leads to emotional equilibrium.

Hartley, Frank, and Goldenson in their book *Understanding Children's Play* have formulated eight functions of play in their detailed observations of preschool children in a variety of settings: (1) to imitate adults, (2) to play out real roles in an intense way, (3) to reflect relationships and experiences, (4) to express pressing needs, (5) to release unacceptable impulses, (6) to reverse roles usually taken, (7) to mirror growth, (8) to work out problems and experiment with solutions.

Other authors and educators have corroborated these findings. Play is no longer considered either as a trivial pastime or as merely a way of releasing energy. Dorothy Weisman in an article which appeared in the *Saturday Review* describes it as "the beautiful central fact of childhood." She quotes Lawrence Frank as writing, "Play is the way a child learns what no one else can teach him."

Mrs. Matterson is in clear agreement with these findings and points of view. She is equally concerned about the nature and quality of play materials and how they are used. She presents a practical guide to selection, arrangement, and use of a great variety of play materials. She states that "play material does not necessarily mean toys." She stresses the value of natural rather than store-bought materials; the delights of sand, mud, and water. She describes mud as a "heaven-sent gift to any child"; and in relation to water, she adds, "It is cheap, easy to provide, doesn't have to be stored, and is extremely satisfying." She alerts parents to the advantages of simple rather than complex, elaborate mechanical toys. She feels that such basic natural materials as water, earth, wood, vegetable matter, rock, and metal "impose a relentless, impersonal, uniform discipline on us all." "If your children were provided with nothing else ever, they would still be far happier and learn more than a good many children with . . . a room full of status-symbol toys."

In discussing dolls, she writes: "There are also those walking, talking, incontinent monstrosities whose value escapes me. Small children need toys—sturdy toys—with which to work out their problems, project their wishes, and on which to imprint their personalities. They are far too young to appreciate the technical magic which makes a doll able to talk, they couldn't care less about a clever gear system which allows an electrically motivated doll to walk a few stiff steps. . . .

"We do them no favor by buying these clever, glamorous toys. They don't understand their limitations and become frustrated by those very 'gimmicks' which make adults want to buy them."

In commenting on dollhouses, she makes a plea for simple structures, rather than the elaborately equipped period type which "leave little scope for the imagination and no room at all for elbows."

She has many excellent suggestions for activities that will interest and occupy the sick child.

Throughout the book there is a recurrent chorus on the value of improvising play materials. Mrs. Matterson is a skilled and imaginative adapter of ordinary scraps. "Any material will do for anything, so long as it serves the purpose." She gives detailed directions for constructing a variety of ingenious toys and pieces of equipment from odds and ends of discarded material. She is equally ingenious in alerting us to the value of exploring the intricacies of nature at work: the delight of children in taking lettuce to pieces and finding the smallest leaves in the middle, of slicing through an apple to discover the seeds and the core, of examining beans and pea pods and their hidden treasures.

Mrs. Matterson also has some very practical suggestions to make about planning play space for children, as well as suitable storage space for toys and equipment. She makes a strong plea for keeping materials in good repair: "Neglected, broken or lost equipment may lead to a narrow choice. Broken items must be mended or replaced, and missing pieces [of puzzles] must be found as soon as possible."

She makes a somewhat startling statement: "All children destroy before they create," which she then elaborates to mean that very young children delight in taking apart or reducing an object to its component parts as a way of understanding it. The opposite of this is also true: that the unstructured "raw" materials (such as blocks, paints, clay, etc.) offer a challenge to children, who, by combining them with their ideas, can produce something uniquely their own, a true creation.

Mrs. Matterson writes less about the value of play in releasing feelings good and bad through identification. She refers to the value of imaginative play as a means of "working out situations and emotions and generally solving infant problems." I feel that this is somewhat oversimplified. Vivid dramatic play is often the means by which young children "play out" rather than "say out" some of the things that are puzzling or confusing or troubling them. Such playing out is often a release of the tension created by fear and anger, but it is not necessarily a *solution* of the problem. This kind of play may provide clues to discerning adults, who will then help the child to understand his problem. This opens the door to action that may lead to solving the problem.

It is in relation to Mrs. Matterson's comments on books and

stories that I found myself in less accord. I cannot agree with her statement that "Fairy stories and fantasies can obviously have full rein but books offering facts to small children should be checked for authenticity."

Obviously, young children should not be presented with stories that misrepresent or confuse. However, I feel strongly that fairy and fantasy stories should be withheld until the child is clear about what is real and unreal. The young child needs to be firmly and comfortably rooted in the world of reality before he can be free to delight in the realms of fantasy and make-believe. Fairy and fantasy tales can be confusing and even frightening to the very young child. They need not be, if he is sure of their nature. Three- and four-year-olds need a story diet of "here-and-nowness" before being exposed to the more glamorous ingredients of the fairy and fantasy world. Fives are beginning to move into this world with excitement and assurance, while sixes and sevens delight in its magic.

Mrs. Matterson makes a good point of the value of using stories (particularly storytelling) as a way of introducing children to new situations which they might find frightening without proper preparation: for example, when going to the hospital, or anticipating a new baby in the family. She suggests using a "mythical child" as the central character around whom the story enfolds, thus giving the listener an opportunity to ask questions without needing to acknowledge the doubts and fears as his own.

I find myself in less agreement with another of Mrs. Matterson's points in relation to children's capacity for listening. She states that her children (presumably preschool age) would listen to Shakespeare being read aloud instead of a bedtime story, and cites examples of other parents who have read long chapters from a physics textbook "without any complaint from the child." Her conclusion is that it is the sound that matters, and that although "children can't understand Beethoven any more than learn physics at the age of three, they like and remember the sound pattern." I suspect that what they really like and remember is the presence and attention of the reader, rather than the sound of what is being read.

Mrs. Matterson also makes a moderate plea for toleration of

comics. "Make sure you don't detest them as at this age children have to be read to." I would add a plea for discrimination in selection if one *must* read them.

Mrs. Matterson's book is a convincing and well-documented description of the importance and value of play and suitable play materials for the best growth and learning of young children. The subject deserves the detailed and serious attention which she gives to it. And the "curiosity, pertinacity, and tremendous energy" of young children deserve the vigorous application of her suggestions.

It is our hope that this "Americanized" version of Mrs. Matterson's book *Play With a Purpose for Under-Sevens* will convey both her concern for giving serious thought to this subject, as well as her ingenious suggestions for enriching children's play. We have endeavored not to alter the text, but merely to substitute American terminology for some of the more British terms with which we are not familiar. We trust that we have not diluted the spirit of enthusiasm that permeated the British edition.

EVELYN BEYER

Introduction

YOUNG PARENTS of today are much better informed about the needs of their young children than their parents were as little as thirty years ago. Information and advice on the upbringing and welfare of children from conception to adolescence is poured into the lap of anyone who reads, listens to the radio, or watches television. Every woman's magazine from the *haute couture* to "this week's pattern inside," from the gay to the dignified, has its special page on family health subjects. The style and content of these pages are geared just as carefully to their readers' needs as the fiction section. There is a similar variation in approach in the large number of books on child care available. We are free to choose as technical or sentimental an approach as we can assimilate.

One aspect of child welfare which is only recently being labeled a problem is the need for suitable play experience before children can develop fully. We have all known and accepted or been told and not accepted that children's early years are vitally important and that they need plenty of things and people to play with. Some experts even go so far as to insist that a child's essential characteristics are irrevocably formed by the time he is five. The "problem" about this phase of development arises because of the changing housing and population patterns. More and more families move away from their home towns and young children lose the easy coming and going of grandparents, aunts, uncles, and cousins without these essential relationships being replaced. Blocks of flats are built higher and higher with no provision made for play space. On new housing estates the dwellings are built closer and infinitesimal gardens are rendered peep-proof, neighbor-proof, child-proof with woven slatted fencing. Streets carry increasing loads of fast traffic and few existing boroughs or districts do much about "play streets." Once children are old enough to go to school they find friends and space to some extent, but what about the preschool child?

Where are these children going to play? Who are they going to play with? What are they going to play with? These basic needs, so simple in themselves, are becoming impossibly difficult to provide: somewhere to run, somewhere to shout, something to climb, a puddle to splash in or a mud patch to dig in, and, most important of all, other children with whom to share the wonderful games and flights of imagination that can change a couple of beer crates into a train, a barrel into a helicopter, a rag doll into a family. These things are our children's birthright. There seems little point in organizing groups and special courses intended to fire adolescents with the spirit of adventure, curiosity, and courage if we stifle these already present attributes in our children at the age of three by not providing scope for their development. It is like opening the stable door when the horse is dead.

Whether we in England are lucky enough to live within reach of a Local Education Authority nursery school or can afford the fees of an independent establishment, there are only places for one child in every hundred. State provision for eighty per cent of the children in the relevant age range as envisaged by the 1944 Education Act still remains a pipe dream.

This provision for play opportunity has to be faced by all parents and is not specific to one income, social, or intelligence group. Those of us who have young children now have to realize that however hard we campaign for more nursery schools or play spaces the results will be too late for our own preschoolers. During the last five years or so many young mothers have decided to provide play facilities for their young children on a do-it-yourself basis. These playgroups are run by groups of mothers who make themselves responsible for hiring suitable premises, providing suitable equipment, and employing suitable supervisors to organize play sessions for their children, the cost being shared on a nonprofit-making basis. Such groups have to be registered with the Ministry of Health and must observe specific rules regarding space, lavatory accommodation, ratio of adults to children, and so on. They vary in size from as few as six children to as many as thirty, some are run in private homes, some are run in community centers, church halls, dance halls—anywhere that the accommodation is judged satisfactory by the local Medical Officer of Health. Some groups are fairly formal like a Ministry of Education nursery school meeting every morning; some are no more than weekly gatherings where mothers leave their children while they do the shopping. The length of sessions is rarely more than three hours either morning or afternoon. At worst they are places where children can be taken to be looked after while their mother does something else. At best they are the ideal environment for the three- to five-year-old children for some part of their day. The standard reached is entirely up to the mother members and the contribution they are willing to make.

However we finally decide to solve the problem of where and with whom our children will play, the question of "with what" is inevitable. All children have the same basic needs and whatever the limitation of the environment, be it permanent or temporary, the same types of play materials are necessary.

As a teacher I was aware of the theory of the value of play. As a young parent I provided for my children much the same things as other parents, using the yardstick of what I liked, what I thought the children would enjoy, and what I could afford. It was only when I became interested in playgroups and play material for numbers of children that I found there was more in this subject than I had appreciated. Books on why children should play were plentiful, as were catalogs showing what is available, but written knowledge on how to combine needs, provision, and environmental limitations was a missing link. Consequently I talked to lots of people who had faced these problems, looked at nursery-school equipment, tried out ideas of my own, and generally approached the subject with rather more respect than it is usually accorded.

The problems of providing play material vary. Nursery schools have to provide for a limited age range but their material is used by generation after generation of children. The toys they have must be strong and, since there is a limit to what nursery-school staff can achieve in their hours of work, most of them must be bought. Fortunately there is the capital available to do this. Playgroups have similar needs but they very rarely have the capital to buy expensive large items. Storage space may be difficult for a playgroup using premises which are not their own so that, even if they have the capital, stock sizes may not be suitable. On the other hand, as a cooperative group they can draw on the free time and skills of parents who can make toys. Parents who have children who must play at home (and whatever we do about nursery schools or playgroups most of the children's time is spent at home) are in the most unfortunate position of all. They have every age range to cater for in quick succession, or at the same time, on a limited income. There are play space and storage difficulties when large items are considered.

After reading, looking, talking, and trying for a considerable time I have come to the heartening conclusion that every environment—homes, nursery schools, playgroups, children's hospitals, temporary homes even—can supply the basic necessities whatever their limitations. After that it is up to the person paying the bill to decide which luxuries to provide.

The secret seems to be in applying the following rules:

Is it essential?
Can you improvise?
Can you make it?
Can it be made to serve two purposes?
Can you store it?
If you have to buy, explore all the possibilities first.
And, most important of all, play material does not necessarily mean toys.

The age range which I have chosen may seem a somewhat arbitrary one but in fact is quite justified. Babies up to the age of three like small things that can be appreciated by their senses without making too much demand on their limited knowledge and physical abilities. Somewhere around the age of three material which offers more scope and information becomes necessary and the toddler starts to evaluate and accept certain basic facts about his environment. After the age of five educational equipment (for want of a better term) is provided at school and sometimes in the home, but up to the age of seven most children still enjoy the material used by the three-year-old. They just do more elaborate things with it.

It would be presumptuous to imply that providing proper play material is all that is necessary—but it is a good start.

I would like to thank all the people who have taken time off to talk to me, given advice, shown me their own equipment and toys, and made suggestions to try out. It would be impossible to thank a specific person for an idea or design. Faced with the same problems many of us have reached similar conclusions, which is surely encouraging.

1

Why Bother?

BY THE AGE OF THREE most young children have learned to walk, talk, and feed themselves and are more or less self-sufficient regarding toilet needs. Their world is still centered around their mother and the people and objects surrounding her. Their relationship with other children is a matter of playing alongside rather than with them, skills are rudimentary, and the attitude to materials is necessarily exploratory. Some time during their sixth year, depending on how crowded their local elementary school is, these same children are required to present themselves to a strange person (along with some thirty to forty other young children) in a strange environment, without the support of the hitherto central figure in their lives, and apply such intelligence and ability as they have developed to the formal art of learning. I am not trying to paint a sentimental picture—merely point out the great progress which must be made during the years preceding school if the transition from home to school is to be a happy one. Nature is on the side of our offspring and has equipped them with all the instincts and attributes necessary to develop their potential. They have curiosity, pertinacity, and tremendous energy. It is our job to see that these instincts are not inhibited by our living conditions to a degree which will stultify development.

Children can only learn from practical experience what things feel like, the results their actions will bring, how other people react to them, and how they react to people. Thus the more stimuli which can be provided and the more relationships, especially with other children and away from the family, the better. The child brought up in an unpermissive household where noise

1

and mess are inconvenient, or where the sole contact with others is provided by his mother, may have great potential he is not able to realize.

Perhaps it is the word "play" which causes a great deal of subconscious inhibition. It can mean so many things, from a rather pleasant but unproductive activity to something positively reprehensible and time-wasting, according to our upbringing. Its truest meaning can be reasonably applied to the process of learning through practical experience and repetition that a young child happily undertakes almost as soon as he is born. His patience and persistence can tire and exasperate his mother even when he is only nine months old. Older children will play for hours fixing one box inside another or dropping stones through gratings or repeating nursery rhymes. In some children this trait can become an obsession in which real distress ensues if exactly the same procedure is not followed day after day for some particular activity such as getting dressed or putting away toys, but this is a rather different problem. Most children lose the love of repetition all too early and they bitterly resent spending time on piano practice, handwriting lessons, or football practice instead of football games.

The seemingly aimless chewing, sucking, or feeling of objects by small babies is their way of coming to grips with textures, shapes, and sizes. Adults can see at a glance whether a chair is strong enough to hold them or whether to bend their heads going through a low door. They know how much effort to put into their actions because they have a fund of experience gained so long ago that they have forgotten how much time, effort, and sometimes physical pain was spent in gaining it.

Small children have to learn what height, depth, weight, and effort mean long before they have the vocabulary to spell it out. They have to learn not to take a knock from a table leg as a personal insult but at the same time to protect themselves and their possessions from animate marauders. Consistencies are a difficult thing to learn and only prolonged practice will gain good results. This is one of the great virtues of playing with mud. While they have fun playing with it the valuable lessons of too wet, too dry, too sticky are imbibed without effort because the sheer pleasure of slip-slopping about is enough to keep them interested.

The same natural discipline is imposed by sand. When my oldest child was two our seaside holiday was made unbearable by shrieks of rage due to sand pies that collapsed or trickled from the bucket during the ritual patting with the spade. The next year he was a bit cleverer and toddled off down to the sea to bring back a bucket of water with which to wet his sand. This time the shrieks were caused by the inevitable loss of water from the bucket, but by the end of the holiday he had learned to walk carefully and slowly. Now at the age of nine he competently finds a bit of beach which is just the right consistency and builds the most complicated layouts of cars, ships, and castles. The shrieks of rage are due now to his younger brother and other small fry ruining his efforts as soon as or even before they are finished. So although the disciplining process is progressing it is not complete even yet. I suppose the lesson he will eventually come to accept is that you just can't win, and which adult would dare to quarrel with that?

One of the characteristics of young children which is a great aid to creativeness is their lack of preconceived ideas. Any material will do for anything, so long as it serves the purpose. Just because strips of perforated metal come in boxes with wheels and pulleys is no reason not to use a single strip as a digging implement in the sandpile—to a small child. By experimenting they reduce objects to size, shape, and possible use without worrying about how much it cost, whether it was made for that purpose, or whether it is spoiling the set to break one piece. Thus they achieve the same simplicity of vision which enabled James Watt to see the significance of a boiling kettle instead of ramming the lid down more securely as most of us would have done. This same "clear seeing" makes nonsense of a good many of our so-called educational toys. Children will learn adult skills quickly enough by using proper tools or implements scaled down to fit their size. Parents can make themselves miserable and inhibit their children by having too many expensive, one-purpose toys about. It drives some people to distraction to see an expensive and attractive toy reduced to useless pieces because an integral part has been used in the making of a rough sailing boat, or to find a rather superior pack of cards made dirty and dog-eared while being used as a load for a homemade truck built of a shoebox and spools. The answer seems to lie in why adults protect some toys and not others and a bit of honest thinking may show we do it for the wrong reasons. Perhaps a toy was expensive, or given by a grandparent who will be upset if it is maltreated. Most likely this seemingly wanton destruction and misuse offends the sense of property and tidiness attained later in life and it would be just as unreasonable to expect children to accept these limitations as to expect them to eat pills which are sugar-coated and not ask for sweets which are sugar all through.

No one would expect a mountaineer to climb Everest without first exercising his mind and body to a pitch where he has a good chance of success, a new recruit in the R.A.F. to fly a jet bomber on his second day, or a schoolgirl to produce a Dior model. These special abilities and skills need a background of personal experience, a degree of skill which enables one to take advantage of other people's knowledge by reading and copying, a fair amount of self-discipline and a well-developed imagination. Even with these attributes it is very rare for a human being to exist or create alone. We need the help and the stimulus of others and unless we learn at an early age how to cooperate and coexist we shall not achieve very much or be happy as adults. The foundations for all these characteristics and skills are laid in the preschool years, and time, thought, and effort should be spent on providing suitable practice (rather than play) facilities even if dividends are a long-term reward. The concern of most mothers is with how they can, with limited time, money, and facilities, do their best by the preschool child without ignoring the demands and rights of the other members of the family.

It is easier to consider play material if we divide play into certain categories (this is quite a false division really, as any good play session will combine elements from all these categories).

CREATIVE PLAY

This is encouraged by the provision of all kinds of raw materials on which the child can exercise his imagination and limited muscular ability. Wood blocks, sand, paint and coloring matter, paper, bits of cloth, and so on all give scope for combining separate materials to make a finished or different object which, while it may have no significance for an adult, can be something very dear and specific to a child. While creating there is also an opportunity to find out about textures, weights, colors—all the basic facts of living in a particular environment. Muscular coordination is gained during creation. Towers built by a two-year-old usually consist of two or three blocks placed laboriously on top of each other with more force than judgment but eight-year-olds can build houses of playing cards. Somewhere along the line a great deal of skill is developed.

IMAGINATIVE PLAY

This overlaps very closely with creative play except there is not necessarily a tangible result. Dressing-up clothes, some object or utensil which will spark off a whole series of situations in the child's mind can be provided or simply acquired by the child himself. During this kind of play he can think himself into situations, work out reactions, and generally come to terms, his own terms, with people and events. The vividness of such play can be frightening to an adult when children appear to live in a dream world with an imaginary companion or have a terror of some imaginary horror. Some children don't learn to differentiate between fact and fiction until quite late, if ever, but this is not a problem of the normal child. As soon as most children have found out how to express themselves satisfactorily in words or actions, painting, music, or dancing, the instinct for imaginative play becomes channeled into suitable activities and they quickly learn what is real and what is not. The bitterest fight I ever had to interfere in was between my then three-year-old youngest son and a two-year-old neighbor. Apparently the young interloper was putting imaginary sacks of coal into my son's imaginary train coal car and blood was drawn before I could calm them down. It wasn't that he minded the coal being loaded but he wanted to do it himself. The final solution was to suggest an imaginary truck so that the imaginary coal could be loaded back and forth. Both the children have progressed since then and nothing less than real coal in a real toy train or truck will do. The protocol and relationship of engineer, truck driver, and who loads what is just as carefully observed but at least the tangible elements have to be tangible.

ADVENTURE PLAY

In its simplest form this is the overcoming of obstacles, mental and physical, and the gaining of new skills whilst exercising every available muscle with such coordination as already exists. This applies just as much to children at play as to mountaineers, yachtsmen, or Channel swimmers. Children gain physically and mentally from overcoming their environment and their delight in climbing, crawling, jumping, or balancing is mirrored in their increasing self-confidence. The countryside provides naturally all kinds of exciting things to do, and we would do well to provide a similar environment. Trees to climb, brooks to jump over, things to lift, stepping-stones to balance on—all these things can be provided for a town child in essence if a little ingenuity is exercised. The great art in this kind of play is to ensure that children do not become discouraged by the obstacles being too difficult or the adult in charge being too restrictive. Small children will attempt only what they can manage and if they think they can climb on top of the sideboard and do a soft-shoe shuffle then they probably can. The fact that such behavior is not acceptable should not prevent some more suitable climbing apparatus being provided. The adult obviously has a duty to ensure that adventure material is intrinsically safe and sound and that something within the child's capabilities is available. After that adventure play can be left to its very satisfactory self.

DEVELOPMENT OF COORDINATION AND
MANIPULATIVE SKILLS

All forms of play encourage these. There are, however, some play materials which are specially designed to help in achieving adult skills such as jigsaw puzzles, color- and shape-matching sets, screw toys. Most of these one-purpose toys lose their appeal when the age of reveling in repetitive activities is passing by. After this proper tools such as scissors, hammers, and screwdrivers are necessary and, while good tools have to be preserved, every child should own or have access to such tools as he is capable of using. Eventually eyes, hands, and brain become so well attuned to each other that the time becomes ripe for children to recognize word patterns and to make small controlled pencil marks which can be guided into letters.

LEARNING AT SECONDHAND

Long before this stage is reached children can be learning by hearing what other people do during story-reading or -telling, looking at books and pictures, or listening to music. I have a feeling we don't give our children enough good music to listen to at the age of three and that we generally underestimate their capacity for listening. Both my children would listen to Shakespeare read aloud instead of a bedtime story and I know other parents who have read long chapters from a physics textbook under similar circumstances without any complaint from the child. Obviously the sound is what matters at this time of day and while children can't understand Beethoven any more than learn physics at the age of three, they like and remember the sound pattern.

This widening of experience at secondhand is essential in our day and age. No one of us could gain enough firsthand knowledge to cover all the changes and eventualities we shall be called on to face in these days of quick and good communication. As far as I can tell television has done my children immense good and no appreciable harm except a tendency to use the catchwords and phrases of the moment and to mutter "Liar, liar" during advertisements. They know far more than I did at their age, sometimes more than I do now, about wild life or true adventure stories, and their general knowledge about past and present is on the whole very wide. Obviously television has its limitations (for instance it needs sensible owners) but as a dispenser of information in an acceptable form it has no equal in my estimation. Its detractors would allege that watching television is a very negative occupation, but at least children learn to look, listen, and concentrate while they are interested. Like every other aid to learning and experiencing it needs to be used in conjunction with all the other material necessary to encourage progress of every kind in the young.

One kind of play I have left until last.

DESTRUCTIVE PLAY

Perhaps it should have come first because all children destroy before they create. Until objects have been reduced to their component parts children cannot understand what they are. If the component parts were not meant to come apart then that is just too bad. Children get great satisfaction from positively changing things into something else. A blank piece of paper can at once be despoiled and yet made into something else by daubing a thick streak of paint on it. One might even consider these destructive impulses to be the first primitive efforts at creation but, however these tendencies are interpreted, there is no getting away from the fact that all children display them sooner or later, to a greater or lesser extent, in their play sessions. The thing to do is to channel such efforts into acceptable behavior without inhibiting activities too much. This is where sand comes into its own—or clay. One can make and then destroy with impunity. No damage done and there is the blank material ready for another defacing. Take-to-pieces toys are useful for this age group if they are properly presented. My eldest son refused to play with a large fire engine which screwed and unscrewed because it was given to him in pieces. Somehow all the fun had been taken out of it and to some extent I sympathized although I thought his reaction a little extreme. We exchanged it for a tractor eventually and this was very much appreciated.

WHERE AND WHEN TO PLAY

Once we have accepted why children need to play, the questions of where and when arise. Even if we are lucky enough to find a place in a playgroup or nursery school, by far the greatest part of a child's life will be spent at home with his mother so it is important to understand and accept the needs of young children. Most of us do, and in fact take great pleasure in playing with our children. But the three- to five-year-old is seldom the only responsibility of the mother. She has a husband, home, and probably older and younger children to care for. All of us are familiar with the situation where finishing off the cleaning or feeding the new baby or getting in the diapers before the storm breaks is genuinely more important than cutting round the difficult bit of the picture on the back of the cereal box. There is no point in feeling guilty or uneasy about this—no household can or should revolve around a three-year-old and if we provide the basic requirements that is as much as can be done without some member of the family not getting his or her fair share of attention.

Somewhere to play is most important. Safe, outside space if possible where children can do messy things, have adventure material, make a noise, and generally let off steam. (A carefully laid out garden will not do!) Inside space is often more difficult but it is only common sense to have one area where children can play with impunity. It may be one special room if there is space, but quite often it has to be a room which is used for another purpose besides and by other members of the family—or other groups. A few rules here are helpful and most children will accept an imaginary barrier around them and their play if adults in turn observe the same courtesies and do not encroach on the play space. Obviously, while part of a room is being used for playing all other considerations have to take second place and it is unfair to grumble about untidiness and clean mess. Really dirty mess and damage is something you have to control or come to terms with yourself. This problem becomes less acute as the family grows and the furniture deteriorates, if that is any consolation to the as yet one-child parents. Obviously there is little virtue and no satisfaction in polishing scratched and chipped furniture. The answer seems to be to refurnish when the children have gone, but then of course there are the grandchildren. . . . Perhaps the choice is even simpler than one realizes: that is, children and a messy house or no children and a satisfactory house. Personally I prefer the children—most of the time.

Play material need not be difficult if one is reasonably ingenious and play-minded nor need it cost a small fortune. More difficult can be the provision of the very best plaything ever devised—another small child. Brothers and sisters are not necessarily congenial playmates although they are infinitely better than no one at all. I have always been fortunate enough to live where the easy coming and going of children was generally accepted, but when the inevitable barren periods have occurred during infectious illnesses or summer holidays my heart has bled for single children who have to be alone, play alone, talk to themselves, fight with their mother who is very likely in the same situation herself with regard to adult companionship. The strain put on the mother-child relationship is released only when the father comes home, which places a heavy onus on a probably tired man who wants only a bit of peace and quiet.

It is over the question of play space, time, and playmates that nursery schools and playgroups really prove their value. If, for only part of the day, a few days each week, children can go off somewhere where there is adequate space and adequate material, to be with other children, and with adults who are concerned only with the welfare of the children and do not have to do the cooking, shopping, and cleaning at the same time, the benefit to child and family has to be experienced to be believed. Children come home with renewed enthusiasm for their own possessions and are delighted to be reunited with the same mother who bored them to tears yesterday. The mother, having had two or three hours free in which to whiz through the housework, go to the dentist, or just have her hair done in peace, is just as pleased to see her offspring, and the activities which go on at the play session are a source of interest to the whole family. New friendships are formed at all levels and children learn naturally the social discipline of belonging to a group at the best possible age.

Specially designed nursery-school buildings always have plenty of storage space and play space but some nursery schools which are run in halls not originally intended for the purpose have to face the same problems as playgroups and homes when it comes to money and storage space. No one could pretend these limitations can be turned into positive advantages, but if they are taken into account right at the beginning they need not be disadvantages. All equipment which can be built on a do-it-yourself basis is useful because it can be tailor-made to fit into the available space. Some equipment can be used for two or more purposes. Certainly the fault of overstocking the toy cupboard with expensive, silly toys does not arise when there is no money to buy a cupboard, let alone contents. Don't let this bother you. The bare bit of wall which is not taken up by the cupboard may be a splendid place to put up a wall blackboard or some other useful piece of equipment.

2

Start at the Beginning

IF YOUR PLAYROOM really is empty you should consider yourself very fortunate. Clearly in such a case one can start at the very beginning and plan exactly what can go where. Not many families or playgroups are as lucky as this. Very few homes have rooms which can be devoted entirely to children's play. In any case few small children will play completely alone in a separate part of the house. So unless there are lots of children to play together or the playroom can be next to where the mother spends most of her time, it is a waste of good space. Older children from five years onward are a different kettle of fish. They love a private place and it is worth going to desperate lengths to convert the attic or clear out the shed to make a den for them.

Halls or rooms viewed with an eye to playgroup use may have to be used by other people and have space taken up with their equipment. These rooms may have trestle tables and chairs in them. Don't despise these often shabby objects. They can be put to splendid use especially by an impecunious group who can't afford proper tables and chairs, or where storage space is short. In Abingdon we ran a playgroup for a whole term without proper tables and even now we use chairs a great deal to support other equipment. Often in the home playroom a couple of chairs facing each other can be the basis of a theater, a store, a fort, a barricade, a cooking table—the possibilities are endless.

Wherever play is to be, and with however many children, it pays dividends to plan the available space carefully. A very large table in a small space leaves no room for moving about. A large cupboard may hold lots of toys but leave no room for playing with them. It is best if play material is available to children at all times, although it is certainly not necessary to lay out every toy or activity at the beginning of a morning. If a number of children are playing together the adults have to decide how many can comfortably play at one thing without interfering with each other and how many different activities should be made available. For children at home games may well be sparked off by what the mother is doing and so will be provided one at a time.

In a playgroup the same basic activities should be provided each day. If more than one game is being played at one time the placing can be important. Nothing riles a small child more than seeing his block tower knocked down by someone else just before he could pull away the bottom block himself. A safe secure space is needed for blocks. A quiet corner is an advantage for reading. Some occupations such as hammering need careful supervision and it is always wise to place them where they can be overlooked without being dominated.

TABLES

Very small children will play happily on the floor for hours, but there comes a time when their legs get in the way and then progress is more satisfactory if they can sit at a table to draw or hammer or do a jigsaw. Working in a specific area also helps to keep the activity within bounds and leaves more room for others to play in. Adult-size tables and chairs may be used but they are not very comfortable for a long game and they take up more space than small-size furniture. If it happens to be the dining table at home there can also be terrible battles at mealtimes when food is spoiling and the game is only half played.

When space is short. Some kind of collapsible table (providing it is safe and solid) is useful, or a simple tabletop to fix on top of a toy chest is a good idea. If the situation is really desperate a couple of planks across two chair seats will serve, but they will not withstand hammering games. For use where a number of tables are necessary, stacking tables of stout thick plywood with tubular metal legs are invaluable. They are extremely strong and half a dozen take no more floor space than one when put away.

The price is also very reasonable considering their length of life. Before we could afford this type of table for our Abingdon playgroup we supported large trestle tables on hampers, one at each end, which made them the right height. Two chairs at each end would have served the purpose had the hampers not been available. There was a major drawback to this, however. Although the trestles were six feet long only one activity could be put on one at a time. If two activities were put on together they became a hopeless jumble which didn't particularly matter except that material could not be used to full advantage and the children became very frustrated. Thus these large surfaces filled the available space without affording working areas for enough activities. They certainly solved the storage problem, however. A similar table half the size might be a useful addition to any playroom.

When money is a problem. It is quite easy to make tables, although here again a couple of planks across chairs can be useful. A very stout table can be made from a sort of upturned shallow tray with lengths of 2 x 2-in. timber screwed into the corners for legs (see Fig. 1). This can be just as solid as you can afford the tabletop timber to be. ½-inch chipboard such as Masonite or plywood is very satisfactory. For do-it-yourself mothers I have come to the conclusion chipboard is rather easier to saw than plywood. Both surfaces need some kind of protection. Either painting or covering with plastic or bits of thick linoleum will suffice. This kind of table is pretty permanent and where storage space is difficult may not be suitable. Alternatively, it is possible to buy ready-made legs which screw into socketed metal plates. Absolutely anybody can make a table with these. All one has to do is cut the tabletop timber to size, attach the special metal plates to the underside with screws, and then screw in the legs (see Fig. 1). The legs can be removed after use and storing four separate legs and a ½-inch thick bit of timber is easy. If you care to dress up the tabletop with leftover linoleum tiles or sheet linoleum and then finish off the edge with a bit of molding, the result can be quite pleasing. (Beginners please note that molding has to be cut with a miter board in order to get a good finish at the corners, stuck on with impact adhesive, and

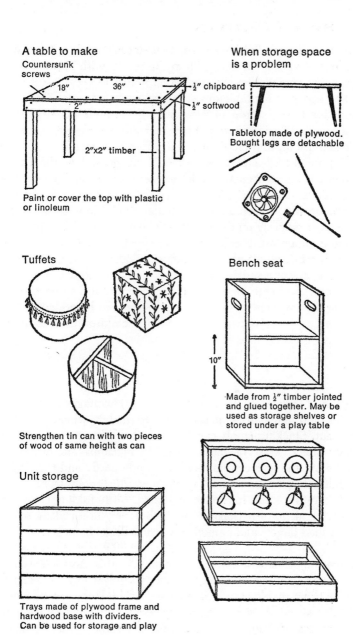

A table to make

Countersunk screws

18" 36"
2"
½" chipboard
½" softwood

2"x2" timber

Paint or cover the top with plastic or linoleum

When storage space is a problem

Tabletop made of plywood. Bought legs are detachable

Tuffets

Strengthen tin can with two pieces of wood of same height as can

Bench seat

10"

Made from ½" timber jointed and glued together. May be used as storage shelves or stored under a play table

Unit storage

Trays made of plywood frame and hardwood base with dividers. Can be used for storage and play

Fig. 1

then nailed with finishing nails. If it doesn't work out too well you can always file it down, fill in the cracks with Plastic Wood, and paint over it. The children won't notice.)

The best size for tabletops seems to be 36 x 18 ins. This gives room for two children to play happily without taking up too much space. Two of these put together make a good-size unit for one activity for four children and works out very well.

The height of a play table should be geared to the chairs. When sitting at a comfortable height, there should be enough room for knees to wriggle a bit under the table. Obviously it is impracticable to keep adding to tables as children grow, so it is wise to err slightly on the big side. The height of things to sit on is more important. It is difficult to concentrate or be comfortable if one's feet are not able to touch the floor properly, and small children are affected by this just as much as adults. Again the problems of growth have to be faced but here it may be wiser to err on the low side. A cushion or pad seat can be added as time goes by. In playgroups catering to many children there is a case for having varied sizes of chairs and tables.

CHAIRS

To buy. Stacking chairs have the same advantages as stacking tables and most firms make them to match which is rather pleasant. Stacking stools can be a boon where storage space is really small. Most of those available in shops are meant for adults but the legs can be shortened quite easily and the rubber feet attached to the new leg end. They are actually more stable, and therefore safer, for being shortened. Little folding chairs are available at quite reasonable prices but they are a likely source of crushed fingers and nipped legs just as deck chairs are.

When money is short. Lack of money in this case is easier to overcome than lack of storage space. Useful little tuffets can be made from padded and covered candy and cracker tins of a suitable size and shape. The tins need strengthening by wedging two pieces of wood at right angles across the tin and packing them in with crumpled newspaper (see Fig. 1). They should be the same height as the tin and will support the lid when it is taped on. A padding of cheap carpet felt, a cover made of stout upholstery material or an old piece of carpet, a bit of fringe or braid for trimming and you'll have children fighting to play Miss Muffet with them, kick them, roll them, hit each other with them, and eventually sit on them. Real emergency can be met by putting a covered or padded plank across a couple of low chair seats or two equal-sized logs or bricks.

When storage is a problem. If someone who is really keen on woodworking is available, small wooden benchlike chairs can be made of ½-inch timber in such a way that they stack sideways and form shelves when the play session is finished, thus fulfilling two needs at once (see Fig. 1). Two-seater versions of these can be made but children usually get on better if they have a chair to themselves. This is an expensive project and, I think, unnecessarily elaborate but it might appeal to some perfectionist fathers.

A cheaper version works perfectly well if you can obtain strong orange boxes or crates, but these serviceable objects are getting more and more difficult to find. After removing dangerous projections, rubbing down and painting with a bit of leftover paint, they make useful storage units. Turned upside down with a padded cushion on the top, they make seats which are the right height for most children (see Fig. 2). Their shape also lends itself to becoming part of a train, a boat, or almost anything the children like to think of.

One of the best buys we ever made for our own children was an old two-leaved kitchen table. The legs were cut down to the right size and the two leaves made into very crude benches by nailing a piece of plank at right angles to each end and giving this a little extra support by screwing a piece of 2 x 2-in. wood into the right angle. These lasted for quite a time and were strong enough to jump or hammer on. Eventually one or more ends came off them and the bits that were left were used as a slide down into the sandpit. The table was left out during last winter and disintegrated when it finally emerged from under the snow, but some of the bits are now incorporated into the rabbit hutch so we really had a good run for our money.

STORING EQUIPMENT

The size and shape of storage space affects all the equipment. If tables and chairs may be left out they can be of a permanent nature. If they have to be put away at the end of the session something which folds, stacks, or is useful as a storage unit is obviously best. Large items such as playhouses may be permanent, or may be made to fold by hingeing the sections, or to come to pieces altogether. If no space is available even for this, one can improvise quite satisfactorily by using a table or chairs draped with a bedspread. By careful planning in our playgroup we manage to stack into a space 9 ins. x 6 ft. the screens necessary to make a 6 x 6-ft. playhouse, a 4 x 6-ft. dressing-up cubicle, a 6 x 4-ft. hospital cubicle, a 4-foot wide shop, and a threefold library screen. (Needless to say they have to be put away in the right order or they won't fit into a 6 x 6-ft. space, let alone anything smaller.) One screen can be made to form two play areas if it closes off a corner of the room.

Unit storage. Whether space is a problem or not, unit storage seems to work much more satisfactorily than having one large cupboard. By this I mean keeping similar playthings or all the material for one activity in one receptacle. It makes for easier setting out and easier clearing up, and lost bits and pieces are soon noticed so that a search can be made before it is too late. If these unit receptacles are uniform in size and shape it facilitates neat stacking and, with a few time-and-motion-study principles applied, the stack can be made quite high.

Receptacles can be filled where the material is and removed to the storage area in various ways. If the floor is smooth a piece of carpet, pile side down, can be used as a sort of skid. If the floor is too rough casters fixed on a flat piece of wood to form a very low dolly can be used. If neither of these methods work one can fill the lowest receptacle where it is to stand, place the empty second one on it and fill that, place the empty third one on top and fill that, and so on. If receptacles must be lifted up after filling it is only common sense to leave the heaviest at the bottom.

These receptacles can be almost anything of a reasonable size, shape, and hollow nature depending on how much money you have, how clever you are, or how good a scrounger you are. There are very superior lockers and units which can be bought, but this seems somewhat extravagant for the majority of us and they don't necessarily suit the shape of the space available. Hampers are perfect. They are robust, light, and easy to handle, stack safely, and when empty make excellent playthings or supports for trestles, play boards, etc. Orange boxes and crates have already been mentioned but strong cardboard cartons will do if the money situation is really tight.

There are lots of things which can be adapted if you keep a sharp lookout for them. In an old-fashioned department store which was closing down I found some of those huge drawers hats are kept in. These would have been capital with a set of casters on the bottom (set in slightly from the sides so that they did not interfere with stacking) and a drawer handle on two opposite sides for pushing and pulling. They would have been a bit heavy when full perhaps but could have been filled in position as suggested earlier. I didn't pursue the matter of these particular drawers because the owner wanted $1.50 each for them but perhaps I was a bit shortsighted. However, there are lots of similar things about. Old-fashioned chests of drawers go very cheaply at sales and could supply the wood to make lockers if they were not satisfactory to use in their existing state.

If storage space is very narrow or long it should be possible to make units to fit. A stack of shallow trays made with a bottom of hardboard and sides of ⅜-inch plywood are useful for storage and can be adapted by putting a division down the middle so that they form shallow shelves when stood on end (see Fig. 1). Such shelving can be used for playing store, playing house (for a china cabinet), bookshelves, or as holders for toy cars and so on.

Shelves to buy. An ideal unit if money and space are not scarce is an open divided-shelf system where toys can be on display although not littering the floor. Children can just take out for themselves what they wish to play with and put it back after the game. Casters on the bottom facilitate cleaning and the unit can

Unit storage

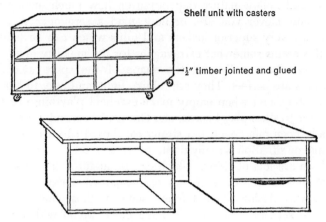

Shelf unit with casters

½" timber jointed and glued

Large playbench with shelves and drawers

Shelving

Making space in a bedroom

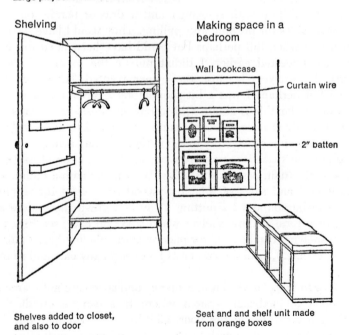

Wall bookcase

Curtain wire

2" batten

Shelves added to closet, and also to door

Seat and and shelf unit made from orange boxes

Fig. 2

also be swung out into the room at right angles to the wall to divide off a play space (see Fig. 2). If it has to stay in a living room and the open front spoils the appearance of the room, a venetian blind or reeded blind would keep things out of sight when down and not interfere with access when up.

Shelves to make. If the playroom being planned is also a bedroom there may be a built-in wardrobe. These are always grown-up height. While children are fairly small the unneeded height can be used at top and bottom to provide shelving right across the back of the closet (see Fig. 2). Since access is limited it is as well to restrict the shelves to a width of 4 or 5 inches at most. They can be supported at the sides by 2 x ¾-in. battens screwed to the wall, which is very easy to do. Anyone with a bit of determination and a good masonry drill can plug a wall. One word of warning. The best of walls are not uniformly perpendicular and in a shelving system from 3 to 6 feet high the necessary length of shelf may vary by as much as half an inch. It is wise to measure for each shelf separately. Don't despair. Any woman who can sew can do woodwork. You just have to be a bit more careful about the measuring and cutting out. The method, roughly, is to saw up the shelf wood to the necessary size, cut battens of the same width and mark on the walls where the battens should go. Drill a hole at each end of the battens. Take one at a time, place it against one of the marked spaces on the wall, and wriggle a nail through the holes so that you mark on the wall where the screws will go through. Label the batten and label the space so that any variations won't botch up the whole job. When all the marks are made, drill the wall with a masonry drill and plug the holes with the correct size of wooden plug. (Ask the hardware dealer about this, they are always pleased to advise.) Push countersunk screws, again of the appropriate size, through the holes in the battens and screw them down into the plugged holes, taking care to match up the right batten with the right holes. Once this is done all you have to do is rest the ends of the shelves on the battens and there is plenty of room for books, cars, shoes, and boxes of unspecified junk. If the closet is wider than the door leading to it you may find it more covenient to use the little recesses at the sides, i.e. across the depth of the closet, rather than the back.

Don't despise places where only a 2-inch wide shelf is possible. Lots of small treasures can be stored on shelves fixed to the back of a door if a piece of molding is fixed across to prevent objects falling off when the door is closed. A series of these looking rather like shallow, elongated spice racks can take quite a fleet of cars or other small toys.

Where bookshelves are impossible, fix 2-inch battens across a wall and stretch a piece of curtain wire across 3 or 4 inches above each. Books can be slipped behind the wire so that their bottom edge rests on the batten (see Fig. 2). This is very good for small children's books as the attractive illustrated covers they have add color and decoration to the room. The battens can be neatened off with a frame of 2-inch timber if the ends do not come up against another wall.

MAKING THE SYSTEM WORK

Once you have decided how and where to store toys you can start considering what and how many they are going to be. It pays to be quite ruthless in discarding or rejecting playthings that there is really no room to play with or store. They become a burden to family and child alike if they are simply a source of knocked shins and frustrated play. An effort should be made to provide the really basic everyday playthings first and to save space and money on the short-lived attraction of one-purpose toys. Fortunately the everyday things such as dough, paint, and water are usually cheap and easy to provide fresh for each session. Unpopular material can either be thrown away, given away, or put away to try out on the next baby, but there is no point in cluttering up the playroom with it.

3

Natural Play Material

NATURAL PLAY MATERIAL is a rather formal term which simply refers to the world around us: water in varying quantities, earth in varying textures, wood, vegetable matter, rock, and metal in all their possible guises. Until we understand and appreciate the properties and limitations of these materials so well we can take them for granted, creation is inhibited and we cannot feel secure within our environment. The instinct to play with and learn to work with these materials is very strong. Adults who do not come into contact with nature during their working hours often choose to spend their leisure time in some activity which brings them in contact with earth, water, wood, or metal. The satisfaction an adult derives from his garden or carpenter's bench started long before he owned his first tools or even had words to express his pleasure. Enthusiasm for Channel swimming probably started in the bathtub of a small baby.

These basic materials impose a relentless, impersonal, uniform discipline on us all. A small child importuning for sweets may get a lollipop or a smack at different times from the same mother depending on circumstances that may not be obvious to his immature mind. He will soon learn that an inanimate bucket of sand produces neither pleasant nor unpleasant reactions. It will respond in exactly the same way to exactly the same treatment every time and results depend entirely on his actions. It doesn't matter how often he kicks a door—it won't open until he does the right things. Getting cross and irritable about lack of results only tires him. The door will still be there next day, equally unmalicious but equally unrelenting. How much better, and less wearing, to let our children learn self-discipline from this kind of material instead of always trying to impose discipline ourselves. The only person likely to achieve any good result would have to be so calm, so impervious, so neutral that these very attributes would make him dull and unrewarding to live with.

WATER PLAY

Playing with water is one of the things babies enjoy even before their eyes focus properly. Its advantages as a play material for any age are obvious. It is cheap, easy to provide, doesn't have to be stored, and is extremely satisfying. Its disadvantages are also obvious. It can be messy, it can be inconvenient, under extreme conditions it can be dangerous. All these drawbacks can be overcome if a few basic rules are borne in mind. It doesn't matter how small the container for water is so long as the playthings are suitably sized. A doll's teapot full of water will do splendidly if the spoons, cups, etc., are small. Boats for a dishpan lake need to be smaller than those sailed in the Round Pond. To provide a 6-foot length of hose is just asking for trouble but a 12-inch piece is very manageable. The water container should be at the right height for the children or vice versa. Children can't manage a saucepan held at arm's length any better than an adult can, but if proper conditions are observed they make very little mess. If the surface on which they are working is suitable or adequately protected a few splashes won't matter. Wiping up spots with a clean cloth specially provided for the purpose can become a part of the fun anyway with proper training. Thus if we think carefully about where to put water play, what to put it in, which playthings to use with it, and how to protect floors and children, absolutely every home, playgroup, or other gathering of children can indulge in water play.

Where to have water play. Weather permitting, out-of-doors water play is most fun because then the activities can vary from all-in-and-splashing-about to pouring cups of tea for pretend picnics or washing doll clothes (see Fig. 3). Hard-surfaced areas are best as grass can get pretty wet and muddy during a good game while concrete and similar finishes dry off quickly. Don't

Sand and water out-of-doors

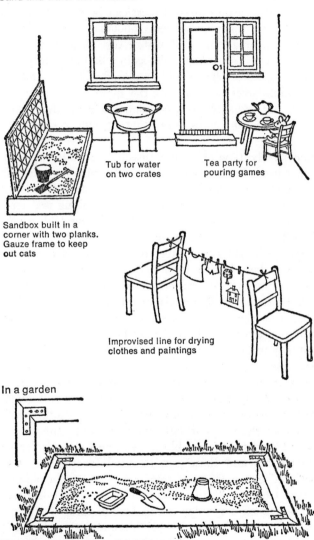

Tub for water
on two crates

Tea party for
pouring games

Sandbox built in a
corner with two planks.
Gauze frame to keep
out cats

Improvised line for drying
clothes and paintings

In a garden

Wood-frame sandpit with metal strips across
corners. Allow 6″ space for foot-room
from top to level of sand

Fig. 3

let grass surfaces put you off, however. They are perfectly adequate and if necessary the wet mess can be guarded until it has dried out after the play session. Indoors it is sensible to have water play near a supply of water; this usually means that a suitable floor surface is available, as in a bathroom or kitchen. In a playgroup, water play should be placed where it can be supervised unobtrusively but out of the main traffic lanes so that accidents are unlikely. It is a quiet, contemplative occupation most of the time and gains from being set slightly apart.

Containers. The type of activity possible depends largely on the container used. Large pools need careful planning and making. Usually they are sunken and lined with concrete. The edges may be concrete, tiled, or paved. Some kind of filling and emptying system is vital and so is filtration or purifying with a chemical solution if the water is to remain in for any length of time and will be used by a large number of children. I feel this kind of provision is best left to large playgroups or local authorities unless you have a large garden and a gardener. It is possible to buy plastic shapes to line pools once the right sized and shaped hole has been prepared. These too need some kind of emptying and filling device but if they are not too large a hosepipe would serve the purpose; they are still a fixed piece of equipment, however, which may not be convenient. An easy pool to provide and store is one of the plastic, pneumatic walled ones which are also cheap. A big wading pool can be used for splashing, boat sailing, and watering-can-like games. A plastic wading pool may be large enough to support only one activity at a time.

Water troughs are available from some toy firms for use indoors and out and these can be used for pouring activities generally. They are made of zinc, can be square or oblong with an area of from 6 to 8 square feet and a depth of 6 inches. They are supported on a wooden frame. One of these would provide scope for between four and six children at a time (see Fig. 4). They are too expensive and large to store for most homes and playrooms. A baby bathtub is just as satisfactory, especially on its stand, as this makes a unit the right size for two small children. A crate or an orange box does quite well for holding

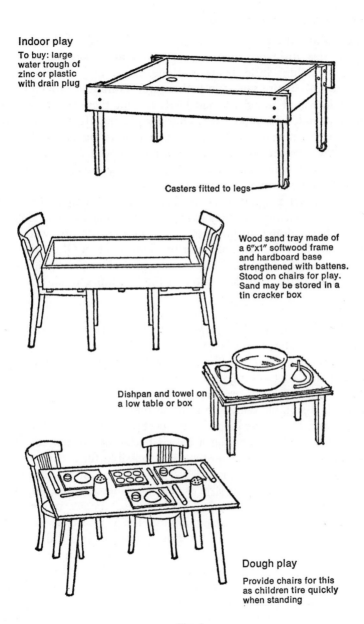

Indoor play

To buy: large water trough of zinc or plastic with drain plug

Casters fitted to legs

Wood sand tray made of a 6"x1" softwood frame and hardboard base strengthened with battens. Stood on chairs for play. Sand may be stored in a tin cracker box

Dishpan and towel on a low table or box

Dough play

Provide chairs for this as children tire quickly when standing

Fig. 4

the bathtub if a proper stand is not available. Baby bathtubs and large size dishpans similarly supported are good for pouring games, sailing little boats, bathing dolls, and washing doll clothes. A car tire sawed in half around its middle provides two shallow round troughs to sail boats in, but these are not to be recommended for indoor use. Outdoor playing after a storm can be fun too if one is not too fussy. A pair of boots, good deep puddles, a paper boat or tin can, a mother who pretends not to notice, and what child could ask for more except perhaps a fast-flowing stream in a nearby gutter?

For indoor playing at home there is no need to go to these lengths. Any child will play happily for hours at a proper sink or hand basin doing all kinds of things or perhaps just watching carefully how the drips of water break off the tap. Of course this means that the sink should be clean, with a chair placed safely in the right place, and that water in the hot tap shouldn't be too hot.

Water playthings. Children will usually choose their own playthings for water, but it is a wise adult who carefully checks and produces something else if necessary. Water for washing clothes can be made interesting by adding a light squeeze of mild liquid detergent, and water for pouring can be colored, but so long as it is made a suitable temperature these refinements are not strictly necessary. Just above blood heat is best and the accepted routine should be as for preparing a baby's bath—always put the cold water in first so that at no time is it possible for a child to get scalded. Pouring equipment is very cheap: a cast-out teapot or coffee percolator if the size of the container permits, funnels, tubes, strainers, pitchers, "squirty" bottles, spoons, a piece of hosepipe. It is worth asking around for very small "squirty" bottles. Plastic fruit shapes are fun. Large-size liquid detergent containers can be cut across the middle to make a funnel and a glass. It is a simple matter to punch holes in plastic glasses or tin cans at different heights and children soon notice and enjoy the effect of water pressure on the resulting jets. Boats can be improvised from walnut shells, bits of balsa, newspaper, leaves, match-boxes—anything light or hollow enough, but there is no need for grown-ups to rack their brains. Children have far more imagination than we have. The only things to ban are glass and sharp, rust-prone metals. One of the most enjoyed games is blowing into bubbly soapy water down a piece of tubing or with a bubble pipe or straw. Most nursery schools and playgroups do this but personally I have reservations concerning cross infection. A dose of a water purifier or antiseptic in the water would probably help to cure adult doubts if nothing else when a group of children are playing blowing bubbles together.

Protecting floors and children. Protection for floors where necessary is most effective when based on the bath mat principle of soaking up as splashes occur rather than wiping up afterward. Layers of newspaper or pads made of old bath towels laid under a baby bathtub or bowl are very efficient. A really precious carpet or floor could be protected with a waterproof sheet of some kind but perhaps it would be better to find another place altogether. Water which slops over the edge of the container could be stopped in its tracks by swathing the sides with a long strip of folded cloth with its ends tightly pinned. All these precautions are really for the adult's peace of mind and they are very rarely necessary if the common-sense rules are observed. Children have much more coordination and control than we tend to give them credit for and most of them have a steady hand if not a strong arm.

Protecting the children is perhaps a little more worthwhile. Water aprons can be bought or made quite easily. I once made seven quite adequate aprons (which are still going strong after eighteen months' wear) from one discarded lady's mackintosh. The variety with a rubber backing on the material is best. One apron from each sleeve, one from each front piece, two from the back skirt and one from the back bodice can be cut out if you are not too fussy about where the original seams come. Straps can be made from the belt and double-faced bits down the front, and the buttonholes and buttons can be used as fastenings if they are sewed on as little separate bits. If this is taking economy too far, strong twill tapes would do just as well. If the aprons are made fairly long they can overlap a pair of boots and there is no need for further worry. A pair of plastic cuffs which are 6-inch tubes of soft plastic with shirring elastic at the top and bottom are useful for protecting the long sleeves of sweaters which always get a bit soggy however far they are pushed up. The height of water-apron luxury is reached if there is an outgrown mackintosh which can be used. By dint of cutting off the collar, removing the belt if there is one, and buttoning the resulting garment on back to front complete protection is effected. The sleeves may or may not be left in but if it is an old mackintosh they are probably just right for playing. There is one advantage to water aprons, indeed to any kind of apron, which is not immediately obvious. If there are only two water aprons, only two can play. Thus the numbers can be limited naturally to whatever the container is suitable for without any need for tantrums, pushings, or shovings. Small children can be asked to wait for an apron rather than for someone else to finish playing and they find this much more acceptable. They can be trained to accept apron protection just as they can be taught to accept clearing up their own splashes as part of the proceedings. In fact, messy water play is due to silly adults not careless children.

We all know about dangerous water play: drownings in canals, pools, static water tanks, reservoirs, germs picked up in contaminated water sources. These are very different problems and as they are localized have to be dealt with as they arise, but the child who can realize his desire to play with water at home in a satisfying manner is less likely to succumb to forbidden temptations of this kind.

SAND

This is a superb basic play material. Dry sand has all the properties of water. Ordinary builder's sand can be used for modeling or pouring, depending on how wet it is. There is no age limit for sand play. Older children just do cleverer things with it and it is a common sight on most beaches to see grown-ups showing as much enthusiasm as their children for sand-castle building.

Buying sand. Sand can vary tremendously in cost—well-washed (to avoid staining) builder's sand of a suitable grade (the builder will advise you on this) is quite cheap. Delivery may cost more than the half cubic yard or so you need. It is also worth asking the builder about the amount. Half a cubic yard of sand will take up a lot more space than a half cubic yard hole when it is being played with. If it is kept only for dry sand play and pouring games it should last quite a long time.

Sand containers. These can be similar to those for water except that drainage should be borne in mind when arranging an outside uncovered pit. These should be lined at the sides only. Sandpits can vary from large, concrete-lined holes to just a heap of sand in a corner of the yard but there are one or two basic rules to observe when planning them. They should be the right size and shape for the number of children who will be using them; an oblong pit is better than a square or round area as each child can have a part to play in without interfering too much with his neighbor. Cleaning up is easier if there is some kind of frame, either wood or concrete (see Fig. 3). Wood must be splinter-free but there is not so much risk of cracked heads as with concrete or paving slabs. Sand has an inevitable tendency to stick to clothes and children and so get into the house; it is a good plan to have a fair expanse of grass or yard in between the sand and back door if possible. If not, a few rules should be laid down about sandy shoes coming off before children come in. A cover of some kind helps if you are troubled by cats. Tarpaulin keeps out the rain, as would a wooden cover, but just to keep out cats a frame covered with chicken wire is adequate. Another point which is worth noting is the advantage of having the level of the edge of the sandpit higher than the level of the sand. At least 6 inches is to be recommended as this means less overflowing and children can sit on the edge in a comfortable position without their knees hitting their chins. Another way to deal with overspill is to have a low wall round the sand but this could lead to accidents.

If the soil in which the hole is to be made is reasonably solid, it is possible just to dig a hole and put in the sand. The edges are rather prickly to sit on and may get a bit messy as time goes by especially if it is used by a large number of children. It depends on how much work you want to do and whereabouts in the yard it is to be. Placing can be important for more than esthetic reasons. Trees may give suitable shade in the summer but can prevent rapid drying out after rain. Easy supervision is necessary as sand games can get a bit rough; therefore sandpits should be within sight of a suitable window. If the only place available is small, a sandbox in a corner will do (see Fig. 3) or simply a heap of sand fenced in with 6-inch wide timber. The fencing will not keep the sand in altogether but at least the sand-playing area will be defined as far as the children are concerned. Any wood used for this purpose should be smoothed and protected against the weather either by painting or coating with a plastic finish made specially for the purpose. Any finish should be checked for poisonous or burning qualities. One can never be sure planks will not be in contact with scratches or even be chewed.

Other suitable containers are zinc bathtubs of varying sizes. These can be sunk, if suitable arrangements are made for covering and draining, or they can be free-standing, supported on bricks or logs. None of these things cost very much except time spent in digging or investigating junk yards. Where space is really hopeless, the same rule that applies to small quantities of water can be applied to sand. I have seen a sandpit made by removing one 24 x 18-in. slab from a paved yard, digging a 6-inch hole, and filling this with sand. It worked very well in conjunction with tiny buckets, spades, and funnels.

Ideally, wet and dry sand should be provided indoors and out. If this is not possible wet sand outside and dry sand indoors is a good compromise. If only one kind can be provided then it is sensible to have just wet sand and let water suffice for pouring play. Indoor containers for sand can be similar to those used for water, placed safely at a suitable height. In addition wooden trays can be made very easily from a frame of wood 6 ins. deep x 1 in. thick screwed at the corners with a bottom of hard-board strengthened by gluing battens across. (It is not wise to attach the battens with nails or screws as they may project and catch fingers as they scrape along the bottom.) The corners can be made stronger by gluing and screwing a bit of right angle molding into the angles. If the joining of frame and bottom is further protected by sticking 2-inch adhesive tape along it, no sand can possibly seep out. These trays are cheap to produce and are useful when storage space is limited. The tray can be supported by the seats of two chairs facing each other and the sand emptied in from a tin cracker box (see Fig. 4). Thus all that is left to store at the end of a session is a 6-inch deep tray which can be stood on its side and a tin box. Obviously this kind of wooden tray is only suitable for dry sand. Baby bathtubs, zinc trays, plastic bowls make good containers for wet sand. If money, space, and storage are difficulties, an ordinary tea tray with a thin layer of sand is better than nothing, providing the playthings are kept small.

Sand toys. Utensils for wet sand can be anything hollow which makes the most of its plastic nature: spades, spoons, shells, buckets made of rubber or plastic, tin cans (preferably painted or discarded as soon as they rust), well-washed ice cream cartons, small pie pans, old saucepans—anything is grist to the mill. It is up to adults to decide what is too big, too dangerous, or too precious and after that children can usually provide quite well for themselves. For dry sand, funnels, sieves, salt shakers, pitchers or tin cans with holes—more or less the same things as are used with water—are suitable.

I doubt if any parent gets through a seaside holiday without buying either a bucket or a spade. Those available vary tremendously and a bit of thought before buying can be time well spent. Plastic buckets have obvious advantages over metal ones and rubber ones are even stronger. Do match the size to the child but don't let the limitations of the local beach shop inhibit the size of your sand castles. Both my children have a one-gallon size plastic bucket that is the envy of every child on the beach. They transport a lot of water, make an impressive castle, and hold a terrifying number of crabs. In addition to all this they cost less than a good many of the overdecorated half-pint sized things one can be fobbed off with.

Spades are rather different. Small children need small spades and rubber or plastic is the safest choice for them. Older children who do what amounts to sculpting can make the best efforts with a large metal one. It is pointless to say that you should inspect the way the metal is fixed to the wooden handle. They are never fixed on well and you just have to choose the best available. It will probably have been lost by next year anyway. Wooden spades are cheap, traditional, safe, and long-lasting but they are too long for babies and scorned by older children in my experience. Do resist those little plastic molds; ice cream cartons and shells do just as well.

Sand play is easy and cheap to provide, is satisfactory however much or little there is room for, and its only disadvantage of messiness can be controlled if children are trained properly, so there is absolutely no excuse for not providing it under normal conditions.

CLAY, MODELING CLAY, AND DOUGH

These other useful plastic materials all differ slightly from wet sand and each other although they have the same virtues.

Clay. Potter's clay is quite cheap or if you are in touch with a pottery class you may well find they can give you supplies of unused mixed clay. A convenient but slightly more expensive way of buying it is in powder form. Local art shops or handicraft suppliers could quote prices for you. Of course if you live in a clay area or near a pottery there is no problem at all. Storage is effected by wrapping the material in a damp cloth and putting the whole bundle in a covered bin. This way supplies can be kept workable for several weeks. Clay and small children are best if nothing except an apron and table protection come between them. They can roll it, punch it, twist it, mold it—you think of it, they do it. There are sets of little plastic hats, feet, hands, and so on that can be used with clay bodies but I have never known this to add positively to the game and it can detract if children fiddle with these things rather than make something different each time. Little pots or animals can be left to dry out in a warm place for a few days and will last quite well if treated gently. Small children, however, are more concerned with the making than the ultimate object and are usually ready to squash up their clay and start again. Clay has one drawback. It tends to spread and as it dries leaves white, streaky marks. They can be wiped off but it is not always convenient to have to do this every time.

Modeling clay. Commercial modeling materials such as Plasticine and Plastalene are similar to clay, are more expensive, and if they spread leave a greasy mess which is very difficult to remove. No special storage is necessary beyond keeping them in a tin.

Dough. If clay is difficult to obtain and you object to Plasticine-type substances a simple and clean modeling material may be made from flour, salt, and water. One pound of plain flour, two ounces of salt, and enough water to mix it to a pliable but nonsticky dough will provide enough for four children. The salt draws water from the atmosphere and keeps the mixture soft. If it is wrapped in a damp cloth or plastic bag or both overnight and reasonably treated in between—i.e. not wiped round the sand tray or peppered with nails or trodden in the flower bed—it will keep for a week. Vegetable coloring matter may be used to make it look more interesting and some people add a tablespoon of olive oil to improve the pliability but it really isn't essential.

Pastry play. Another use for this flour mixture is pastry or dough play (see Fig. 4). This is quite a different activity from modeling as utensils are used to roll, cut, and shape the material just as mothers do when baking. Pastry boards are not strictly necessary, but again they help to define areas which prevent children spreading too much. They can be an offcut of wood or hardboard suitably protected with paint or varnish (nontoxic, or course), a bit of plastic covering left from doing shelves, or an odd linoleum tile. Rolling pins may be bought but a length from the end of a broom handle is the right diameter and just as good. Large salt shakers make efficient flour sifters, or a small tin can with holes in. It pays to be a bit mean about the number of holes, so a homemade version may be best. Every cutlery drawer contains tea knives which couldn't cut if their existence depended on it and these poor blunt objects will delight any small cook without being a source of danger. Tin lids, plastic plates, and old pie pans make good cake tins and those silly little cutters that are too small for normal use are just right for pastry play. Forks and spoons are useful to make pretty edgings, even lollipop sticks can be utilized, but here again it is more to the point to examine and limit what the children provide rather than use your own imagination. All these things, including the plastic bag of dough, can be kept in a cracker box if the boards and rollers are made the right size and this is very convenient for limited storage.

While playing with these pouring and molding materials children learn about textures, shapes, and tensile strength, they exercise muscles and eyes, improve coordination, and at the same time let off a lot of steam. It is much more satisfactory to bang a piece of clay with half a block than beat the new baby with it—from everybody's point of view. Scope is given for destructive play without any damage being done if proper precautions are taken from the beginning.

WOOD

Another natural material which is a great asset in the playroom is wood. Its characteristics vary from those of plastic material and, indeed, one type of wood differs very much from another. Activities can vary from block building with commercial or do-it-yourself blocks of suitable sizes to hammer play with bits of orange box.

Blocks. If you have a cheap source of wood nearby and a keen handyman, blocks can be made very satisfactorily. Generally speaking children enjoy large blocks most as progress is more impressive than using tiny 1-inch cubes. Really large blocks should be made hollow, otherwise the weight might limit play and make clearing up harder work than it need be. Plywood or a mixture of plywood and softwood is suitable for hollow blocks. A job lot of offcuts from a builder or lumberyard would be a good source of supply. Size can be just as large as will be convenient to store but it is sensible to decide on a basic size and then produce whole block, half block, quarter block, double sizes, and so on. Arches and bridges to match are difficult to provide but suitable sizes of flat pieces of plywood are very good for roofs, bridges, and ramps. If only half a dozen of these large blocks can be provided and stored it is worth making the effort as they can be used in conjunction with other things or alone. A good basic size is that of the ordinary domestic brick; or a 6-inch cube would make for easy measuring. Corners can be jointed but it isn't really necessary. Their very shape adds strength and gluing with impact adhesive and fastening with nails (the size will depend on the thickness of the wood) should be quite adequate (see Fig. 5).

If you have enough money there are some excellent sets of blocks to buy. They are expensive but last virtually forever. Sets of colored cubes are useful for young children but most older ones prefer the plain polished wood blocks which come in a variety of basic shapes and have their own duffel bag container. Other types are those shaped in such a way that their interlocking properties enable more elaborate towers to be built. Some toy shops and most educational suppliers provide hollow wooden blocks of varying sizes and shapes but they are much too expensive and bulky for the average parent to buy or accommodate. In addition to these plain blocks there are many kinds of picture blocks, fiddly little shaped blocks with pictures of windows or doors and the like, but once they are made so elaborate they must be taken out of the natural wood construction material class and discussed elsewhere.

Carpentry. This is a delightful occupation for small children but it must be carefully and constantly supervised. Very young children manage best with softwood and may have to wait awhile before they can manage a saw, but most four-year-olds can, with the help of a vise and a sympathetic adult, produce quite a creditable aeroplane or ship. The first thing they all make is a dagger or sword but whether this is because the shape is simple or for more aggressive reasons one can't tell. A safe solid surface is needed for hammering. A bench is ideal (see Fig. 5) but if this is impossible the floor, properly protected, is better than a rickety table. Plasterboard is very good for protecting tabletops and floors but care must be taken to have the plasterboard rather

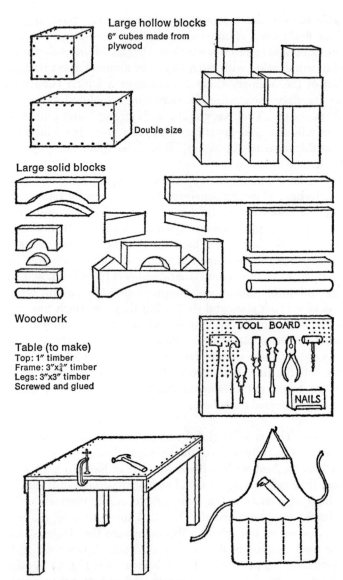

Large hollow blocks
6" cubes made from plywood

Double size

Large solid blocks

Woodwork

Table (to make)
Top: 1" timber
Frame: 3"x¾" timber
Legs: 3"x3" timber
Screwed and glued

TOOL BOARD

NAILS

Edging on short sides fastened inside legs
to give a ledge for clamps, vises, etc.

Fig. 5

thicker than the nails provided as it squashes on impact. Use two or three layers if necessary. For learners plasterboard is good fun by itself as large-headed tacks go into it easily and then one can remove them with pliers or a lever of some kind. This presupposes that a constant supply of board is available as it gets messy quite quickly. Little colored wooden shapes with holes in are useful too as they can be fixed in a pattern by hammering nails through their centers. These may be bought or made by drilling holes in shapes bought as mosaic which are slightly thicker and so more durable. If you are just hard up for something to do or money is short, it is an easy enough matter to cut shapes from colored cardboard and punch holes through these. They can always be replaced at the cost of a little time and effort or the children can do it themselves, which is even better.

Providing tools. Tools should be small-sized but good. Nothing infuriates a child more, or is more dangerous, than a silly little hammer whose head flies off, or a saw that wriggles about as it is being used, or pliers that don't grip properly. Proper small-size hammers and other things are available and should not be prohibitively expensive. Those delightful planes made like graters are good for children and mothers alike and make a useful addition to any toolbox. Vises are essential if sawing is to be undertaken and must be fastened to something firm while in use. Most of them can be removed for storage. Again a smaller version of the proper thing is much better than a so-called toy one. My personal opinion (although not everyone would agree with me) is that children should be taught respect for tools as soon as they are old enough to use them. This is easy if some kind of ritual is observed about putting them away and putting a drop of oil in the right places occasionally. It won't be a drop and it won't be in the right place at first but it is worth persevering. Putting away is less tedious if a proper place is provided for each item. A suitable box may be lined with layers of plastic foam cut so that tools fit into the right-shaped hole. Thick things like a vise might need a hole cut from six or seven layers while a shallow saw may need a hole in only one layer. The easiest way to do it is to fill the box with as many layers of foam as necessary. Lay the tools on the top layer and draw round them. Remove the top layer and cut out these shapes. Replace it, put in the tools and, if they still project above the top as most of them will, draw on the second layer of foam the shape that needs to be cut out, and so on until each tool has a close fitting nest into which to fit. Another put-away gimmick, for that is all they are really, is to have a hanging board with nails on which the tools may be hung and to draw or paint the outline of each tool where it hangs on the board (see Fig. 5). This way children know at a glance what is missing at the end of the game. If it is not convenient to have the board hanging up, elastic loops fastened through holes could be used to anchor the tools at their ends; then the board can be laid flat. This proper concern for tools should not be allowed to delay children in learning which and what size tool is for which and what size job. They soon come to realize that a small pair of pliers has its uses even if it is not so impressive as a larger pair.

A proper concern for small children on the part of adults need not prohibit woodwork for the under-fours. A good rule is that the smaller the children the bigger the nail and the softer the wood must be. If even a 3-inch nail does not give enough safety factor between hammer and finger, the nail can be pushed through a strip of stiff card and the card held in the hand until the nail is well bedded in the wood. Cardboard cartons are fun to saw although this needs an eye kept on it and the results are not very elegant.

Providing wood. The local lumberyard would probably be glad to let you have a sack full of interesting bits and pieces of wood for very little, and the odd shapes will help to fire the imagination. Orange boxes or other crates can be broken up and the pieces used if they are not too splintery. They provide practice for using a sandblock, i.e. a bit of sandpaper wrapped round a matchbox or small piece of wood. A magnet kept in or near the nail box helps to prevent spills and their consequences, although the nails may be somewhat difficult to separate. Any inducement to picking up is worth a bit of inconvenience, however.

Woodwork aprons help to limit the number playing at any one time and this is more essential for this activity than any other.

These can be fun if pockets are made to hold tools, but since they won't hold all the tools it is usually more convenient to have a special box for storage at the end of the game. A further luxury is to keep a pot of poster paint and large brush available for painting finished woodwork. If these are kept in an old baking pan, the painting can be kept under control quite easily and it is a good thing to learn the habit of finishing off a job well as early as possible.

UTILIZING HOUSEHOLD MATERIALS

There are other household materials which could be used alone or as part of another game for special reasons or special occasions. Bran, for instance, has some of the properties of wet sand and dry sand. Although it isn't quite so good as either, there may be a time when it will do. Sawdust is very similar. Dried peas, beans, rice, lentils, or barley can all be used alone just for the fun of handling, measuring, pouring, and counting or they can be used with dump trucks and cranes as loads. None of them needs more than sweeping up at the end of the session and, if you are clever, children will enjoy this part of the game too. A lump of block salt placed on layers of newspaper can be hacked, sawed, hammered, rolled, and generally mauled about for quite a while by a reasonably competent two-year-old-plus but one has to keep a weather eye open for cuts and scratches before producing it. The real value of these things is to produce a change now and then or when ordinary play material is not available—for instance, during a visit to grandparents. Not all of them are retrievable, but neither are they expensive.

Those delightful little cowrie shells, ghosts from schooldays for most of us, can be bought quite cheaply and have lots of uses. A supply of shells may be brought back from a seaside holiday if you can bear to wash them thoroughly and if transporting them is not the last straw for an overloaded car or father. Buttons, strictly speaking, are not a natural material but they can be used in so many ways which have nothing to do with their original purpose that they just about qualify for this heading. Dead match-sticks in quantity, empty matchboxes; absolutely anything found in a home can be used as play material if your eyes are properly attuned.

MUD

There is one more play material which is a heaven-sent gift to any child, yellow, black, red, or white from any walk of life and any part of the world. Mud! Please think carefully before banning it. It isn't necessarily messy if properly controlled and it costs nothing, is obtainable anywhere with outside space, and gives immense pleasure and satisfaction. It is the impromptu mud games that are inconvenient. If children are properly dressed up (perhaps I should say down) with old clothes and boots, and understand that water supplies must be fetched from the kitchen at the beginning, not in the middle, and appreciate that they must keep to a given area, then I don't see what can go wrong except a mud fight; and that can happen at any time, perhaps when the children are not dressed for it. We have had a mud pit for some months now as the last time all the sand disappeared from the sandpit the children decided mud was just as good and the sand would do in a pile. This means that all the slip-slopping is done in a small area, and a plank put across it to serve as a support for mud pies prevents too much getting on the grass. All the old saucepans, pitchers, kettles, and receptacles find a happy home here and the sand spades from the beach are put to good use. Just one word of warning. For the sake of neighborly relations it is better if you find out first whose mother minds and whose doesn't. Peering through the bars of the gate is the only safe place for children who are not allowed.

None of the things mentioned in this chapter need cost anything, be difficult to find, or messy to use. If your children were provided with nothing else ever, they would still be far happier and learn more than a good many children with inconsiderate parents and a room full of status-symbol toys.

4

Providing Opportunity for
Imaginative Play

As its name suggests, imaginative play exists largely in the mind and needs very little tangible material. Its greatest value lies in providing scope for working out situations and emotions and generally solving infant problems. This eliminates the need for words or advanced psychological recognition that is beyond the vocabulary or understanding of a three-year-old.

The most important aids to successful imaginative play are time and tact on the part of the mother. A tactful mother will give suitable warning about a proposed change of activity so that plenty of time is left to finish off whatever it was. This can be difficult if the activity is not obvious, but it is worthwhile taking the child just as seriously as he takes himself. Exposing him to the indignity of scorn and ridicule can hurt a three-year-old just as deeply as an adult.

Young children work off a good deal of emotion during play which is a useful safety valve. It is much better for a jealous three-year-old to beat an old rag doll to shreds than bite, scratch, and kick another child. The make-believe teacher of six will bully, beat, and boss her make-believe pupils who all enjoy it immensely. They just cannot decide how to portray the voice of authority without using violence, mental or physical. Some adults never develop beyond this stage—we all know the petty official who delights in bullying, the schoolteacher and nurse who are far more fierce than is necessary or desirable. If young children can be allowed time, privacy, and a few props, they practice and try on for size all the situations and attitudes that will occur later in life.

A private little place can be a great boon to a small child. I use the word "little" literally. If we think of a world in which tables came up to our heads, chair seats came up to our middles, and other human beings towered twelve feet above us, imagine what a relief it would be to get into a small space we could cope with at our own level. This is why children make a den behind the settee or insist on playing in a small recess in the kitchen.

PLAYHOUSES

These are the answer in the playgroup and the home if there is room. They can be elaborate little buildings, with a roof, door, and curtains or simply a folding screen which separates off part of a room. It is best if they are high enough for an adult to see over but not for a child to do so; especially when a number of children play together. Children get distracted by being able to see what the other people are doing. Four feet is a good height.

To buy. Where money, play space, and storage are not problems there are some good screen-type playhouses to be bought. The best are units which can be fixed together. Each unit has one feature, either a door, window, or hatch so that it can be almost any building the child has a fancy for—a house, store, or theater. Another type is a strong plastic, or fabric, tentlike shape which fits over a doweling frame. Those I have seen seemed very dark and miserable inside and did not leave much scope for other than house play, but this type of thing could fill a need. More necessary than overelaborate designs with a roof and fancy porch are simple play fittings inside. There is some delightful wooden equipment made by one or two firms such as dressers, stoves, mangles, ironing boards, etc., which are well made and designed although expensive. The same firms make strong and esthetically pleasing dolls' cots which they advertise as being potential heirlooms and I can well believe it. It is important that such items will withstand reasonable strain and, for the amount of money they cost, I feel they should actually work, i.e. doors should open and close, knobs should turn, etc. All these things can add to the quiet absorption of playing house but they should not be overdone.

Many other things spring to mind for use with house play: cutlery, crockery, brooms, etc. Always buy a small version of the proper thing if it is available. The good toy shops offer strong, safe playthings but one should avoid flimsy articles which will break easily. It is frightening and disheartening for a small child who is not always sure how much force to use to find things breaking in his hand. A good criterion is either to let the child imagine he is using things or to let him actually use them in a proper manner. Something in between is neither satisfactory play nor good training. Cups, jugs, and teapots should have handles little fingers can grasp properly for instance and cutlery should be child-size, not doll-size. Equipment for dollhouses is a very different matter and I shall mention this later.

To make. Screens are easy to make, can be designed to fit into the play space available and of such a size as to fold and store satisfactorily if necessary. The same rule applies to height as for bought screens. If you use a corner a twofold screen will make a complete little room or a threefold screen placed a few feet away from the corner will give two semi-enclosed play spaces (see Fig. 6). Many arrangements are possible and it is worth making a scale plan before rushing out to buy wood and a saw. The screens must take their strength and rigidity from either the frame or the main material. Hardboard, for instance, is relatively strong and quite adequate if a frame of battens is fixed to it. Corrugated cardboard, cheap linoleum, or painted canvas are not so strong and durable and so need a more rigid frame. These last three materials are useful if the screens have to be carried or lifted any distance for storing as they are much lighter than hardboard. Work can be saved if the sizes in which basic materials come are borne in mind during planning. 6 x 4 ft. is the size in which hardboard usually comes so if your playhouse screens are made 4 ft. high x 6 ft. wide or 3 ft. wide there is less cutting to do than for a screen 3 ft. 9 ins. x 5 ft. 6 ins. If peculiar sizes are unavoidable, I can tell you from bitter experience that it is safer

Arranging screens

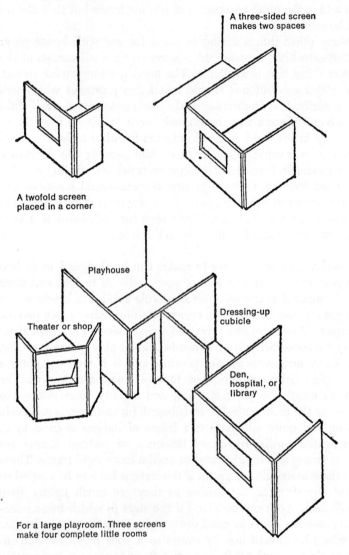

A three-sided screen makes two spaces

A twofold screen placed in a corner

Playhouse

Theater or shop

Dressing-up cubicle

Den, hospital, or library

For a large playroom. Three screens make four complete little rooms

Fig. 6

to pay a little extra and have the board cut to size. Canvas, linoleum, and cardboard also have basic widths.

Once you have decided on the shape, size, and material you can plan which, if any, features such as doors or windows shall go where and whether or not the pieces should be fixed rigidly together, hinged, or made to separate completely. In all cases I would advise hingeing (see Fig. 7) but a simple joining of pieces, using metal eyes in each piece so that they overlap and a bolt fixed through both, works quite well. Hinges may be ordinary metal ones screwed to the batten frame or made of carpet binding wrapped and tacked around the adjoining side battens rather like those on an old-fashioned clotheshorse. The pieces of binding can be wrapped around the battens before the frame is covered with or attached to the main material. If they are to be put on afterward it is necessary to make a small slit in the main material alongside the batten so that the binding can be slipped through. If the screen is 4 feet high there should be at least three hinges at each join whether metal or tape.

Screens made of hardboard can be cut to shape first and the battens applied by sticking them on with impact glue and then stapling. Joints which bear any weight or strain such as outside corners or a door frame should be properly jointed with a half butt joint (see Fig. 7). This means marking where the two pieces overlap, chipping or sawing away half the wood from each so that they fit snugly together, and then gluing and nailing the pieces together. If you are not sufficiently expert or brave to try a half butt joint, another method is to measure and glue the battens so that they touch, then apply a right-angled piece of perforated metal (like outsize Meccano) and screw it down to both pieces. Joints which are not so vulnerable can be effected by measuring the battens carefully so that they fit into the necessary space exactly and hammering in a corrugated clip so that half is in one batten and half in the adjoining one (see Fig. 7).

A 1-foot square piece of hardboard is quite rigid; a 4-foot square piece is rather bendy and a 6 x 4-ft. piece is positively whippy. Any length over 4 feet needs stiffening not only along its edges but by placing additional battens parallel with the long

Making screens for playhouses, etc.

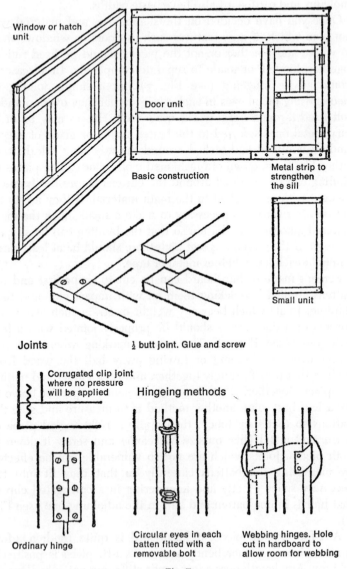

Window or hatch unit

Door unit

Metal strip to strengthen the sill

Basic construction

Small unit

Joints

½ butt joint. Glue and screw

Corrugated clip joint where no pressure will be applied

Hingeing methods

Ordinary hinge

Circular eyes in each batten fitted with a removable bolt

Webbing hinges. Hole cut in hardboard to allow room for webbing

Fig. 7

edges to keep it rigid (see Fig. 7). The piece of batten which makes the bottom part of a door frame and forms a sill should always be strengthened by screwing a piece of perforated metal along its length. This can be obtained from a garage or hardware store. If it is made just high enough to ensure that the door cannot be opened the wrong way, it will save wear and tear on the hinges.

Screens made from linoleum, canvas, or cardboard can be made to the same design as hardboard but the framework must be made first and the covering material tacked on afterward. All joints should be very strong to keep the frame rigid and if this is done there is no reason why such a playhouse should not last just as long as a heavier one. One can always replace the covering. Pieces of a cot or playpen might make a useful frame basis. A clotheshorse covered with material is a cheap way of providing a screen for any purpose and will do quite well for a playhouse.

It is inevitable that screens will be moved from one place to another and apart from making them light and hinged or seg-mented for easy storing and moving there is one more trick which is a help: less energy is required to push these pieces along than lift them. If the floor is polished, it is enough to pad the bottom edge of the screen with the coarse binding meant for coco matting. This makes a tough skid surface and lasts for a long time. If the floor is rough, a narrow piece of wood (4 x 8 ins.) fitted with two casters can be slipped under each end of the screen and is easier and safer than attaching casters to the screen.

One very good idea is a set of large hardboard units compris-ing squares, rectangles, right-angle and equilateral triangles with a module or basic size of approximately 2 feet. These can be hinged or joined very simply by threading a piece of wired tape through holes and twisting its ends to secure it. Many different arrangements are possible for making low houses, boats, trucks, or what have you that are of sufficient size for children to sit in. One could not make a child-height playhouse of them but where space and storage are limited a set like this would be most useful.

Furnishings. Playhouse furniture can be made very easily (see Fig. 8): a stove from a small cupboard with gas or electric heating

Equipping the store

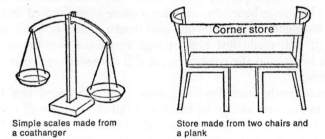

Simple scales made from
a coathanger

Store made from two chairs and
a plank

Equipping the playhouse

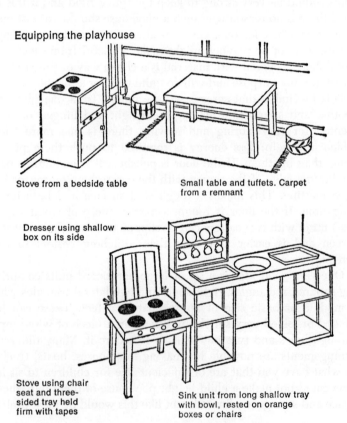

Stove from a bedside table

Small table and tuffets. Carpet
from a remnant

Dresser using shallow
box on its side

Stove using chair
seat and three-
sided tray held
firm with tapes

Sink unit from long shallow tray
with bowl, rested on orange
boxes or chairs

Fig. 8

elements painted on top, a simple dresser from one of the shallow boxes mentioned in Chapter 2 with a divider being used as a shelf. Where storage space is difficult chairs can be utilized by making shallow, three-sided, upturned trays to fit over the seats. Tapes from the back corners fastened round the chair frame make them less likely to tip. One of these trays can be painted to look like a stove top and bottle caps can be nailed to the front edge to serve as switches. A long tray fixed over two chairs with a 12-inch space between them can have a hole made in the middle so that a small dishpan can fit in, and you have a sink unit that takes very little storage when the chairs are stacked away. A similar long tray placed over an orange box at each end makes an even better sink unit and the boxes can be used as storage units afterward. Tuffets or stools as mentioned in Chapter 2 can be used in the playhouse and a small table is useful. Try nailing a piece of timber 12 x 2 x 2 ins. into each corner of an upturned tray for legs and covering the top with a bit of linoleum. This is quite adequate for the purpose.

A bit of carpet in the playhouse is useful because a child can sweep it just as her mother does. Raw edges may be bound with adhesive binding or a remnant of carpet fringing. All this is unnecessarily frivolous, however, and only applies to those who enjoy trimming things.

To improvise. Where money and storage space are hopelessly inadequate the best thing to do is see what can be done about making a little corner somewhere or, more likely, making it possible for a small child to keep the corner he has chosen for himself. For a large number of children an adequate screen may be made from chairs with their seats facing in to be used as play surfaces, and their backs covered with old bedspreads, curtains, or sheets. It doesn't take long to arrange and all that has to be provided and stored is the fabric. A similar arrangement can be made in a corner with pieces of a disused cot or playpen lashed together to form a frame to drape with old curtains.

Orange boxes can be utilized for stoves, cupboards, seats, or tables, or a strong cardboard carton will suffice for anything but sitting on. Everything else can be borrowed for the day from the grown-up cupboards.

HOSPITALS AND DENS

Hospitals and dens are exactly the same as playhouses except for the contents. In a home there is only need for one little house or screen as one child can decide for himself which game to play today. In playgroups there is a case for separate screens if possible. As I mentioned earlier, clever placing can give two spaces for the price of one and their proximity means that one can be used as a natural adjunct to the other; a pretend accident in the playhouse can be taken next door to be treated in the hospital. We live in clinically, medically, and surgically minded times. Not counting injections for this, that, and the other, it seems reasonable to suppose that every one of us will have some kind of hospital experience sooner or later. If we include dental treatment the possibility becomes a certainty. If small children can familiarize themselves with white coats, caps, and "shots" by playing hospital with a group of other children or a family of dolls, they are less likely to be apprehensive of the real thing.

Bits and pieces for playing hospital are easy to acquire. A folding cot is useful—ideally it should be large enough for a child to lie on—but failing this a folded blanket and pillow laid on the floor would do. A table and chair are not essential but would be welcome. Stethoscopes may be bought at toy shops. Here again it pays to buy the strongest version you can find. There are "Doctors and Nurses" kits packed in a medical bag containing imitation instruments of every kind. Such elaborate toys might become the pride and joy of a particular child but in my experience they have a very limited appeal. A stethoscope, some bandages, and a few Band-Aids are enough for most children. Nurses' uniforms comprising a simple white apron and a hemmed square of cloth large enough to fold into a headdress are easy to make or improvise. If everybody wants to be a nurse at once, one can make a few caps out of folded paper bags and paper clips and safety pin plain tea-towels round the children's middles, but limiting the number of uniforms available can be a good idea. It helps to ensure that someone will be a patient while waiting for a turn with the apron.

PLAY STORES

This is another game which is a natural activity for small children. By imitating their mother they are sorting out the social give-and-take they overhear during shopping sessions and learning the rather complicated procedure of choosing and paying for the necessities of life. Very little children will play with pretend things but the older ones enjoy one or two simple objects. No household lacks for wrappings and cartons of all shapes and sizes in our overpackaged environment and if they are resealed with sticky tape an interesting store can be gathered and replaced as necessary. A small basket, bag, or other container, a few bottle caps or other disks to simulate money, and the game is on.

To buy. Screens bought for a playhouse can be used for a shop if a small hatch or window unit is included. A set of small bookshelves will provide display and storage facilities.

Cash registers are fun and some toy firms offer good strong ones, but they are expensive. Imitation coins made of card, plastic, or metal can be obtained from the same people, but again are costly. A toy telephone is also appreciated for shop use. Scales are a great delight. The ones with proper weights are expensive. It is worth having some that work reasonably well so if there is not enough money to buy good toy ones perhaps you can find an old pair of proper ones. They go quite cheaply at sales. A screen or counter is not strictly necessary but can add to the fun.

To make. For a large number of children or where space is plentiful it is pleasant to have a special shop screen. It can be made in the same way as playhouse screens, to fit wherever necessary, but it is enough if the screen is simply a façade with wings to ensure stability, rather than a complete room. A large opening for a hatch and a counter which can be kept in the horizontal position by chains or let down flat for storage works very well. Additional display and storage can be obtained by using the shallow storage trays mentioned in Chapter 2.

A good shelf unit can be made from a collection of shoeboxes which either are the same size or fit together adequately. They can be stuck together by gluing or using sticky tape. All shelves and dividers will then be of double cardboard and the whole thing is surprisingly strong. A local shoe shop will be delighted to give you a pile of boxes if you ask.

A crude but effective set of scales may be made by using a hookless coathanger as a balance arm with a small round baking pan suspended by cord or chains from each end and the center pivoted on a forked rod fixed into a heavy base (see Fig. 8). This is less cumbersome than a pair of old-fashioned scales and cheaper than toy sets.

To improvise. The only essentials for playing store are goods, space over which to hand them, and somewhere to display them. Trading in the East is still done from the ground by a vendor sitting cross-legged on a cushion. Who are we to demand counter and display units? The odds are, however, that your child won't accept this point of view so, if you can spare a couple of chairs, put them together so that their seats form a counter and their backs frame the sides of the "shop"; goods can be stored under them—thus every need is fulfilled (see Fig. 8). The ubiquitous orange box, carton, or shoebox, also serve a useful purpose. Full cans or packages can be borrowed from the grown-up cupboard at a pinch and cardboard money is very easy to cut out. Everything else can come from the ordinary toy box.

THEATERS

Toy theater equipment can vary from a primitive arrangement over some kind of counter to the elaborate buildings of wood or cardboard which have colorful scenery and lighting systems. The essential function of any theater equipment for preschool children is to provide a focus for puppet activities. The younger the child the simpler this equipment should be. As a rough guide, the three-year-old just needs some kind of puppet through which to project his thoughts, the four-year-old enjoys the limited formality afforded by a simple stage, and the five-year-old will appreciate curtains or a screening arrangement which will help to define the beginning and end of the "show" or game. Thus for the preschool age an elaborate theater and puppets should be left severely alone. Simple equipment can be provided easily.

To buy. Any of the playhouses already described which have a hatch or a shop screen with a frame around the serving counter can be used. Pretty material mounted on a length of curtain rod is adequate for curtains. Some toy firms produce a special puppet theater screen which is essentially a three-sided booth, having a let-down hatch in the middle screen which serves as a stage. The height (about 4 feet) is sufficient to screen the child from view. The whole lot can be folded flat for storage. The prices are more than most parents would want to pay and indeed more than is justifiable to spend on a piece of equipment with limited possibilities. A simpler arrangement is a "table theater." This consists of a three-sided screen to place on a table so that the table surface is used as the stage. The middle leaf of the screen is little more than a frame with a rod for curtains fixed across the top. The side pieces project backward to enclose the stage area (see Fig. 9).

To make. Any of the theaters available for buying can be copied quickly and easily. Apart from the advantage of costing next to nothing, they can be made of such a size as will suit your storage and play space. The same principles apply as for playhouse screens with regard to battens, frames, and hingeing. When planning the size, enough width should be allowed to enable a child to move his arms freely and enough height to prevent him seeing over the top whether it is a free-standing or tabletop version.

To improvise. Most children will fix up an adequate stage for themselves if they are left alone. You could give them a start by putting two chairs together as for shop play and producing a cloth for a curtain. A table placed across a suitable doorway is simple and effective. If you have an orange box to spare, odd bits of wood may be added to form wings and a proscenium arch. Use the orange box with the long side horizontal. Nail side pieces

Theaters

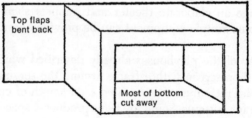

Top flaps bent back

Most of bottom cut away

Made from a carton

Improvised puppets

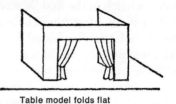

Table model folds flat

Made from tin can with ice-cream carton hat

Puppet to make

Paper bag with cat face and drinking-straw whiskers

Glove fitted with circular head over middle three fingers. Buttons and collar added last

Fig. 9

to the square sides so that they stand up to a height of 2 feet above the top surface. Nail another piece of wood across the top of these side projections to make a frame. Stand the whole lot on a second box and the height is right for most children. Or you can use an ordinary carton with the top flaps folded out of the way, or cut off, and most of the bottom cut away to leave a narrow frame (see Fig. 9). When all this is placed on a table the puppeteer can sit behind it and perform with his puppets within this cardboard box frame. If a bit of colored wrapping paper or wallpaper is used for decoration it is a great improvement. The whole lot can be thrown away at the end of the game thus solving the storage problem, so there is absolutely no reason why any child can't play puppets.

PUPPETS

These may mean a number of things to a child: a companion, a mouthpiece, an outlet for behavior which would be disapproved normally. Some children have soft toys which fulfill all these needs but a puppet is easier to manipulate than a dear but clumsy Teddy bear. Hand puppets are best for the preschool child.

Bought puppets. There is a wide range in price and type and most parents will find something to suit their taste and pocket. Price is no guarantee of a good finish in my experience, so examine them carefully before buying. The problem is finding one which fits a small hand. A fairly loose fit is necessary if the fingers are to move freely but this can lead to a too-large-all-over fault which makes handling difficult. A new type of hand puppet is a sponge rubber animal head shape made so that a hand can be put inside and the face screwed up, stretched wide, or generally twisted about to quite horrific effect. The price is much the same as for glove puppets and they are very good.

Making hand puppets. This is better than buying puppets because they can be made in a suitable size. To make a pattern for the ordinary glove shape with two "arms" and a "head" which is

moved by the forefinger and two middle fingers, draw round
your child's hand when the thumb and little finger are out-
stretched, being reasonably generous. When cutting out this
shape in material allow a specified amount for seams and be sure
to stick to this when sewing up. The head can be made of a
lightly stuffed cloth ball fitted over the three-finger piece while
someone is wearing the glove. Make sure that the fingers can be
stretched to their full length before tacking the edges of the ball
to the base of the three-finger piece. The head can then be
painted, embroidered, or otherwise decorated with features and
hair (raffia, wool, string, felt strips, fur may all be used). Do any
decorating of the glove part before sewing up.

A papier-mâché head is more ambitious but briefly consists of
a pulped mixture of newspaper and wallpaper paste pressed
round a ball of oil-based modeling clay and pushed into shape,
leaving a neck opening big enough for three fingers. When
it is thoroughly dry the clay has to be scooped out, so that
one is left with a hollow head which can be attached to the
three-finger part of the glove. An inflated balloon can also be
used as a base. A clever father could carve a balsa wood head on
the same principle—but at the age of five such elaboration is
really unnecessary.

An absolute natural for puppet making is an odd glove fitted
with a felt head over the middle three fingers (see Fig. 9). It fits,
it is comfortable, and it costs less than an ice cream cone to
make. The easiest way to make the head is to cut two circles of
felt or cloth about 3 inches in diameter. Stitch or stick these
together round their circumference leaving a 2-inch gap which
will be the neck hole for the three middle fingers to go in. Mark
in the features, stuff it very lightly with kapok or cotton, and,
with the glove on, tack it or stick it firmly so that the forefinger
and two middle fingers go through the 2-inch gap and are thus
enclosed by the face part at the front and the head part at the
back. It should be possible to move the three fingers together but
not spread them out. Arms are represented by the thumb and
little finger. Hair can then be applied and perhaps a collar and
other bits and pieces. To vary the puppets simple shirts may be
loosely attached at the neck and arms. Once you have got the

hang of it there is no need to stick to a plain round-faced head. If you can't make up suitable shapes, have a good look at the animal faces on the backs of cereal boxes or in children's comics.

Improvised puppets. If you have no money, can't sew, and your children are meticulous about not losing gloves, or if you are far from home and the toy cupboard, there is fun to be had from paper bags and rubber bands. Paint a funny face on a paper bag and attach it to a fist with a large rubber band round the wrist. If you can find only small-size bands use a hankie or a ribbon fairly loosely tied. A suitably sized tin can or carton can be painted and placed on a fist. At absolute rock bottom, such as a railway carriage or a car full of exasperated grown-ups and bursting children, try inking faces on thumbs and fingers. It won't endear you to other passengers but at least it creates a diversion.

5

Conventional Toys Which
Aid Imaginative Play

ONCE YOU HAVE PROVIDED a place for imaginative play, the
next necessity is a few simple props to aid or stimulate the
imagination. Most of these, whether homemade or bought, are to
be found in every toy box. More money and space can be wasted
or saved in providing these things than any other toys. There are
many catalogs available from shops and manufacturers and a
little time spent in choosing the right toys for your needs is well
worthwhile.

FAMILY PLAY

It is perhaps oversimplifying and -classifying to separate family
play from playhouse play. Often they occur together, but at one
extreme we have small children pretending to play house and at
the other they are making dolls play house. Somewhere in between comes playing with dolls. Dolls and their equipment loom
so large in a small child's life that they deserve a section to
themselves.

Dolls to buy. There is such a bewildering variety of dolls available that we should think, before buying, which kind will fill the
present need (unless children ask for something specific; to give
a Raggedy Ann when a strong-minded four-year-old wants a
"bride" doll is to court disaster). Dolls to play with vary in shape,
size, style, material, and dress more than any other single cate-

60

gory of toys but basically can be divided into baby dolls with which a child can play being a mother or father, and those which are made to resemble children or grown-ups in features and clothing. Thus in theory one can provide either a baby, a companion, or for older children something which projects an image of how they may look and dress as teenagers.

Modern technology has made dolls of all kinds tougher and more pleasant to handle than ever before. One can wash hair, dislocate limbs, and poke eyes with impunity. It is impossible to say quite flatly which age group appreciates which type of doll. I remember one small girl telling me about the "bride" doll she was having for Christmas. When it finally arrived I thought it hideous but she thought it was the last word in elegance and saw nothing incongruous in pushing it round in an apple box carriage with a tea-towel for a cover and a broken down old Teddy at the other end. So—you will have to make up your own mind. Does your child want a baby, a companion, or a practice figure, will she enjoy dressing and undressing it, is she more interested in the clothes that go with it? Once you have decided the type, you can go on to how much you can afford to pay and how big it is to be (to fit in carriage, cot, or whatever). By this time you should be ready to look around the shop. You can now decide which you think is strongest and well made, whether you like the face, coloring, and hairstyle, whether its clothes are well finished and can be put on and off easily. Be ruthless and demand a demonstration if these points are not immediately obvious. You will have driven the shop assistant into a frenzy but if you are lucky you will have found one from the collection which fits your particular bill. It is rare for a child to have just one doll, however, and more likely than not she will end up with a selection which covers most categories.

In addition to the main groups of dolls there are the figures which are dressed in national costume or those delightful little wooden dolls which children love to receive and never play with. The reason is obvious. One can't "do" anything with them, only look, and this is not much use to a young child.

There are also those talking, walking, incontinent monstrosities whose value escapes me. Small children need toys—sturdy toys—with which to work out their problems, project their wishes, and on which to imprint their own personalities. They are far too young to appreciate the technical magic which makes a doll able to talk, they couldn't care less about a clever gear system which allows an electrically motivated doll to walk a few stiff steps, and they haven't enough coordination or experience to realize which fabrics are delicate and need careful handling. We do them no favor in buying these clever, glamorous toys. They don't understand their limitations and become frustrated by those very "gimmicks" which make adults want to buy them.

Dolls to make. Dolls are fun to make. Most homes have the raw materials necessary for sewed or knitted figures and it is a good way of using up odd bits of material. One can buy delightful patterns for dolls or soft toys and their clothes and there are one or two excellent little books on the subject.

If you observe one or two basic principles it is easy to work out a pattern for yourself. You can then knit the pieces or use cloth as you wish. The head when finished should be as wide as it is long; the body should be the same width and one and a half times as long. The arms should be half as wide and one and a half times as long as the head; the legs should be half as wide and twice as long as the head. The easiest way to achieve this is to work out the measurements, make one long sausage for the head and body, divide off the head from the body by sewing a narrow band tightly around to make a neck, then stuff both ends. You can use kapok, synthetic pillow stuffing, or chopped up foam rubber. Old nylon stockings cut into tiny pieces are admirable. Stuff firmly but not rock hard. Run a gathering thread round the top edge of the head piece, pull it up tightly, and sew the edges together. Turn in the edges of the body piece and sew them straight across to give a square end. Thus we now have the front and back of the body defined. Sew up the four stuffed sausages which make arms and legs and attach them to the body very firmly (see Fig. 10). Draw around the relevant bits to make patterns for clothing. Do leave generous openings and add a bit extra for "ease." Features and hair can be the do-it-yourself variety or bought, as you wish. Wool and candlewick cotton are good for hair. Long strands can be laid across the head and stitched down to make a "parting"; this is quick and easy. The ends can be braided or tied in a pony tail with a ribbon. A few discreet stitches here and there are a good investment. Curly hair is effected by couchstitching loops of darning wool, twelve at a time, all over the head. This takes an enormous amount of wool and is tedious to do but looks good and lasts well. Embroidered features last well. It is worth planning what you are going to do on a piece of paper before you start.

Dolls to improvise. Don't waste another thought on this. The children are quite capable of rolling up a towel or enclosing a bit of screwed-up newspaper in the middle of a towel and calling that the head and the folds the body of their "baby." A packet of pipe cleaners can provide a small family in no time.

DOLLS' EQUIPMENT

Here again I have made a somewhat arbitrary distinction between items which relate to dolls and are doll-size rather than child-size although some, like doll carriages, are for dolls to fit in and children to use.

Doll carriages. If you are buying a doll carriage you are faced with almost as wide a choice as buying dolls. Some are good, elegant, ridiculously expensive, some are bad, clumsy, and ridiculously expensive. The best thing to do if your child desperately wants one of these elegant shiny versions is to look for a secondhand one. They are always in good condition—after all, who is going to let a child play properly with something so expensive and eminently scratchable? With luck you should get away with half price and a good polish. Failing this, a quarter the original price and a tin of paint. If there is a large family of small girls it could be argued that an expensive doll carriage can be handed on. From my experience they all want a carriage of their own and I would feel tempted to buy two secondhand ones for use at the same time if there is room to store them. If storage is difficult, find doll carriages which have fold-down handles.

If you do decide to buy a doll carriage explore all the possibilities before you choose and then examine the one you finally buy. Insist that anything mechanically or otherwise wrong with it is put right before you leave the shop, or choose another one. Do match the size of carriage to the size of child. Obviously the child will grow, but it is not much fun to have a new toy that is too big to play with when it is given. Ill-judged gifts may come into their own after a time, but there is never the same delirious happiness associated with them as the right thing at the right time.

My own choice, especially for use with a large group of children, would be one of the strongly made all-wooden doll carriages. These are simple in shape, the right size for small children, and there is little to go wrong either mechanically or otherwise. They are also cheaper than good metal ones.

The same kind of care should be exercised when buying dolls' strollers. These are cheaper propositions than carriages but they don't give so much scope for the tucking in of pillows and covers that is the main attraction of a carriage. If storage space is limited they may be easier to deal with, however. Some fold quite small.

Making a doll carriage is difficult if you wish to achieve the same looks and finish as one of the bought metal ones and is not really a practical undertaking. If you can find an old child's stroller wheel base (or even just the wheels), then with a sturdy wooden box to make the body and the old handle shortened somewhat, you are getting on toward having a reasonable substitute (see Fig. 10). A hood frame can be made from metal strip or wood and may either be permanently fixed in the halfway up position or made to concertina up and down like a real one. Covering material can be any fabric that is strong enough: sailcloth, drill, tough upholstery fabrics.

Covering a fixed frame is easy. Stretch the material tightly over the frame, making pleats or miters where necessary and wrap the edges firmly round the framework. Tack or sew it in position and it should last quite satisfactorily.

Folding frames are more difficult and it is wise to cut a paper pattern first. Cut a strip wide enough to cover the center section

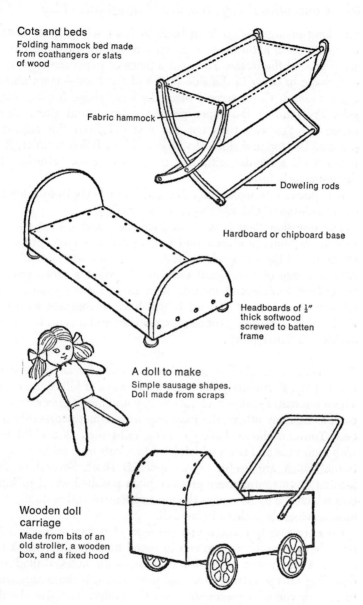

Cots and beds

Folding hammock bed made
from coathangers or slats
of wood

Fabric hammock

Doweling rods

Hardboard or chipboard base

Headboards of $\frac{1}{2}''$
thick softwood
screwed to batten
frame

A doll to make

Simple sausage shapes.
Doll made from scraps

Wooden doll carriage

Made from bits of an
old stroller, a wooden
box, and a fixed hood

Fig. 10

and long enough to go from back to front when open. Leave adequate seam allowances, especially where the material has to wrap around the frame. Then cut a piece of paper the right size and shape to cover in the side pieces of the hood—again allowing for seams. Cut a second piece the same shape for the other side. Try pinning the paper on to the frame and alter where necessary. You can then cut the material from the adjusted pattern. The top and sides can be joined by a felled seam or, if it is too thick, a regular seam and the whole lot then attached to the frame as before.

It is possible to make the axles and buy wheels from a toy or hardware store if old wheels prove hard to find.

The question then is will children enjoy and accept even a well-made home-produced doll carriage? For a large group of children and the young child they are ideal and are appreciated. After the age of five, small girls usually want a more grown-up-looking vehicle and include it in their big toy priority list when writing to Santa Claus. It will have to compete with the rival claims of bicycles, toboggans, watches and it is up to you to decide its relative merit.

Dolls' cots. Some kind of cot or bed is a must for any version of family play. Fortunately there are many ways of filling the need. There are many varieties of cots to buy and many prices. In this case, as in many others, the most expensive is not necessarily the best. You can choose basket cradles, cribs such as a child has with high rails and sides which let down, cots on a folding metal frame which are useful where space is short. Several of the leading toy manufacturers produce plain polished wood rocking cots which are by no means the most expensive and certainly the most serviceable without being dull.

Cots are easy to make if you are short of money and it is only sensible to save where you can to spend on things that can't be made. A cot made of a strong frame with holes drilled for doweling rails is a straightforward proposition. If these are made to fold or come to pieces so much the better. The size should bear some relation to the child and the largest doll it will have to accommodate, but as a rough guide 20 ins. high x 24 ins.

long x 15 ins. wide is large enough to allow "tucking" room round a fair-sized doll. The frame which supports the mattress should be placed about 12 inches from the ground. This will be a bit high for small children and a bit low for a big seven-year-old but is a reasonable size for the longest possible time. A cradle-type cot can be made from a narrow, deep wooden basket covered with material. These last a long time especially if you take the trouble to add spool feet or cut a couple of coathangers to make rockers.

A doll's bed can be made by gluing and nailing a batten frame around a piece of hardboard (plywood if you think it will be sat on, chipboard if you know it will be jumped on) for a base and attaching ½-inch softwood or plywood head and foot boards by screwing them to the battens at top and bottom (see Fig. 10). If the headboards are slightly shaped by rubbing off the corners or having the top edge slightly wider or narrower than the bottom edge, and painted, so much the better. All it needs now is feet. Again spools come in useful or large round wooden beads look rather sweet. Failing these, building cubes or just blocks of wood will serve the purpose. These beds are not so easy for a small child to manage as tucking in bedclothes is more difficult.

Folding cots are easy to make and useful. One can either use slats of wood or two pairs of coathangers bolted together 6 inches from their ends to make the end pieces which fold out or in. The end "crosses" then have to be joined together by a length of doweling (20 inches is a good size) from each arm of one cross to the corresponding arm of the second cross. The bed part is made by making a fabric sling or hammock, with a square gusset at head and foot, which hangs down from the top dowels. The square gusset should be large enough to allow the crosses to open wide but not so wide as to cause complete collapse (see Fig. 10). If you wish to drape it try an old nylon petticoat, preferably one with a frill.

Cots can be improvised from anything hollow and the right size and shape. Most houses have a shopping basket whose handle has come to pieces, an old suitcase which can have its lid removed, even a shoebox or carton will do. If you cover up raw edges with wallpaper or a piece of cloth they need no other trimming. If you are away from home a deep-sided tray would do at a pinch.

Doll's bedding is fun to make and uses up lots of odds and ends which are too large to throw away. There are one or two basic rules to observe. It should be washable, large enough to tuck in, and well made. Pillows and mattresses may be stuffed with foam rubber, chopped-up nylon stockings, or any synthetic pillow stuffing. Satin eiderdowns won't last long but a pretty print trimmed with coarse lace is very serviceable. Old nylon underclothes are a good source of frilly bits and edgings. If you have to provide bedding for more than one cot or carriage or both, it is a good thing to make different matching sets for each. This won't mean a thing during play sessions but it is a great help when finding all the bits to launder or put back where they should be.

Dolls' clothes. If you have to buy them, apply the same rules as for buying your own: will they fit, is the fabric good, are they well made—after all, size for size, you will have to pay a lot more for dolls' clothes. Either knitting or sewing for dolls can be done with the aid of patterns which are good and plentiful once you have found one to match the doll size. If you make patterns yourself, leave enough allowance for ease and make huge openings with snaps. The simpler the shape the better, but interest can be added by sewing on collars, bows, pockets, pretty buttons, or lace edgings. Once children can manage scissors they may be left alone with pinking shears, a stapler, and the piece bag. Boys and girls enjoy this so don't automatically exclude boys from doll play. It is a great mistake to label types of play as "sissy" or "tomboyish" according to which sex is doing it, but it is one of those peculiar attitudes which die hard.

Dolls' furniture. By this I mean furniture which is doll-size not dollhouse size. It is possible to buy wardrobes, dressing tables, dressers, crockery and cutlery, tables and chairs in a size to fit quite a large doll. Some of them are well made, some are not, but all are expensive. If you have the money and are prepared to spend it on these attractive but unnecessary items, then choose the best made at the most advantageous price. If you like making things and think your child would enjoy having these luxuries, most of them are simple to make although fussy and tedious because of their size. A transformed apple box or crate for a table, a block of wood or a tin can padded and covered with fabric for a seat, and a double wardrobe made from an orange box with pieces of doweling fixed across to take small coathangers (made of bent wire) are more than adequate.

Dollhouses. You can obtain a dollhouse in Queen Anne, Tudor, Regency, Ye Olde Cottage, Red-brick semi, or any other style you like and you will be asked to pay anything up to forty dollars or more for it. If they were accurate and authentic in detail this would mitigate the enormity somewhat but they are not even that. They leave little scope for the imagination and no room at all for elbows. Even when the whole front or roof comes off, access is limited and they are usually decorated in a stereotyped manner which leaves no option as to where the furniture is to be placed. Furniture may cost you more than five dollars a set and even if you buy units it is still very expensive. The difficulty of making small objects partly justifies this. Molded plastic things are cheaper but break easily and are not esthetically pleasing on the whole.

If your child desperately wants one of these fanciful mansions then do try to make one or buy one secondhand. If you have no decided views to contend with, there are two types of dollhouse that, after a disheartening day spent looking at the others, had the same effect on me as a ray of sunshine. One was a prize-winning design in a toy-designing competition and is an open-sided dollhouse in which only the central or inner walls are present and the sides are completely open (see Fig. 11). There are eight rooms, four below and four above so that at least two children can play with it at the same time. It is sturdily built, of pleasing proportions and a good size, may be taken to pieces and reerected and does not cost the earth when compared with some of the other fragile follies. The other good design is a set of plain units, little more than boxes, with the top and one side left open and a door or window in each of the other sides. The units then

Dollhouses

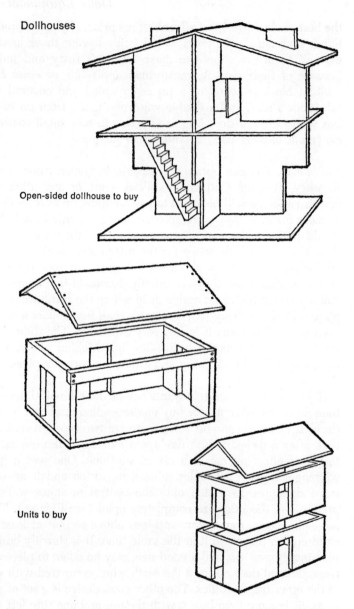

Open-sided dollhouse to buy

Units to buy

Fig. 11

fit together with a roof to put on the top (see Fig. 11). As they can be bought separately, one could add to them as necessary or able. These, too, are plain and sturdy but pleasant to look at, and not prohibitively expensive. Some of the dollhouse furniture is good but as I suggested earlier you are more likely to be restricted by your pocket than your taste. This is another profitable field for do-it-yourselfers. Tiny dolls to go in the dollhouse come into the same category.

Making dollhouses is a natural for the handyman. There are patterns or kits to buy but designing one is not difficult. Leave plenty of open sides to give full rein for rearranging furniture and err on the side of plainness rather than overdecoration. Children are imposed upon by the limitations of their own home. Do give them a little freedom in the house in which they can be the boss.

Solid furniture can be built up from shaped pieces of wood stuck together with impact glue. This method is suitable for rather square armchairs, sofas, beds, etc. Hollow furniture with doors or drawers which actually work is difficult to make and it is easier just to paint detail on. Papier-mâché is a good medium for making shaped objects such as a lavatory basin, tub, toilet, sink, etc., if you make a modeling clay core. Balsa wood may be carved and although it will dent is strong but light for difficult shapes.

You will probably have more ideas on improvisation from watching your children than I can give, but a series of shoeboxes with holes cut in for windows and doors will provide at least one afternoon's enjoyment. Cereal or other cartons used as thick walls and stuck together to make rooms or units last well. Paper doilies cut up for lace curtains are effective and a piece of wool fabric with its edges frayed into a fringe makes an adequate rug. A tree made from a pencil lapped round with green paper fringe or plastic foam and stood in a spool will represent a garden. Plant pots made from suitably shaped bottle caps with plastic flowers embedded in modeling clay soil are fun to make and play with. Matchboxes are invaluable as furniture either for sets of drawers when made into a six-box unit with bead handles or fixed together to make an armchair shape. Tables may be made from a round cheese box stuck to a spool pedestal; doors cut in tea cartons will give a crude cupboard. Add a few figures made from pipe cleaners and the house is well equipped. By the time all these things have been made and decorated it will be time to pack up, so playing with them can be deferred until tomorrow and you thus have two good games instead of one. They don't last long which gives an opportunity for another inventive session.

DRESSING UP

Anyone who has seen a small girl dressed in her mother's hat, a long lace-curtain skirt, and a pair of high-heeled shoes, carefully pushing her baby down the walk will know how a well-stocked dressing-up box adds to imaginative play. Sometimes dressing up is enough in itself, sometimes it is part of another game such as house play, sometimes just an extra fillip rather like using a long cigarette holder for special occasions. For the first kind of dressing up one should provide interesting clothes, pretty hats, petticoats, lace curtains to be pinned across the back and wrists to make wings or fastened round the head as a veil, pretty shoes, and jewelry. Handbags, shopping bags all add to the fun. Boys enjoy capes, hoods, daddies' ties, vests, hats, and Arab headdresses made of curtains, or a toga arrangement fastened round with an old tie or pajama cord. A good supply of safety pins and a helping hand can transform an old bath towel into almost anything. Newspaper will do at a pinch, especially for hats.

Dressing up for a game needs slightly more specific material. Some bought sets are very elaborate but will please a child who has set his heart on all the bits and pieces. In most cases one only needs to provide one feather headdress for a whole tribe of small boys to start playing Indians (the other headdresses can be made from paper) or one policeman's helmet to start off a game that lasts at least three weeks on and off. One battered bridal coronet is sufficient to furnish several wedding games, coronations, or ball sequences, all inextricably mixed but highly enjoyable to the players and observers alike.

Making a cowboy or Indian set, nurse's outfit, or any other

kind of uniform presents no problems if you make a plain loose-fitting garment in an appropriate color and add the signs of the trade. Thus a plain blue smock topped with a white apron and as simple or elaborate a cap as you can manage will do for a nurse. Add a red or blue cross to the bib. A white shirt worn back to front would be adequate for a would-be doctor if there is a large pocket from which to dangle a stethoscope. Indians need a smock tunic well fringed and trousers to match with a fringe down the side seam. Pheasant or turkey feathers make a head-dress. Sterilize them either in the oven or in an antiseptic solution. When they are dry stick them into a 2-inch band of material with a suitable adhesive. Cowboys can wear much the same as Indians but you will have to buy a hat. A felt bolero can be put on top of the shirt and if you pink the edges and add small pockets well studded with brass paper fasteners or rickrack braid, it looks most effective. If you do buy a cowboy set or have one given, it is important to avoid those wide trouser side-flaps that are so common. As most cowboys these days are tricycle-mounted these floppy trousers present a serious hazard. They get caught in chains and spokes. For the same reason I am never happy to see a bride with a lace-curtain train pedaling for all she is worth to join in a fight or some other interesting gathering. The rule should be laid down firmly—no long clothes (not counting tight trousers, of course) on a tricycle or bicycle.

If you can obtain old army, air force, or navy caps these are a source of ideas; and bus-driver, engine-driver, meter-man caps are all useful additions to the dressing-up box.

Even more detailed than "profession" symbols are costumes in which the child dresses to be someone or something special. It is possible to buy and make costumes like those worn by television, comic, or book personalities and puppets. All they suggest, however, is the kind of activity carried out by the particular personality and thus are limiting as far as proper imaginative play goes.

Not quite in the same class are animal costumes. If playing pussy is limited to a hood incorporating ears and whiskers and to a tail suitably pinned on, then this is a good idea. If it involves getting into a fur snowsuit affair with elaborate paws, claws, and glass eyes, it is not. Children are satisfied just to be a cat or bear and don't go on to being an animal who does interesting things. Should an old fur coat, jacket, or other suitable garment be available for cutting up, it would be far more profitable to make several balaclava helments with ears, snouts, or what have you so that several children can play, rather than use it all on one full suit. Cut a paper pattern and try it on before you cut the material (see Fig. 12). Cardboard animal masks (copy basic ideas from those rather good ones on the backs of cereal boxes) can be cut out by the children and with elastic loops to go round the back of the head will last at least as long as the game.

Adhesive tape or a bit of burnt cork are great assets to the "makeup" tin but it is wise to limit the amounts available and replace often.

The secret of keeping an interesting dressing-up box is to provide plenty of raw material in the shape of curtains, sheets; fastening things such as pins, ties, pajama cords; pretty hats, shoes, and jewelry; lots of symbols (e.g., badges, armbands, caps) to represent one particular profession. These should be changed as often as possible or practicable. Used in conjunction with a simply furnished makeup box and a supply of cardboard to cut up and paint, there is not much an inventive child won't manage with a bit of help. Remember the children are dressing up to their satisfaction and they are willing to take far more for granted than adults.

What to keep all this stuff in? A special drawer or box, hamper or carton, trunk or suitcase will all serve the purpose. If a space can be set aside for dressing up, especially in a large playroom with a number of children, so much the better as the contents of the box can be laid out on show. This is easier than delving into a big container as some things might never emerge from the bottom. One absolute must which may not be obvious until it is pointed out is an available mirror—preferably full length. Half the fun of dressing up is lost if you can't see the effect. Second-hand shops would probably have one if neighbors and relations can't help, but it must be made safe and secure wherever it is used and kept. A dressing-table made from a skirted orange box, or a tray top tied on to a chair seat as described in Chapter 2 and having a gay frill thumbtacked in pleats under the edging, add

Dressing up

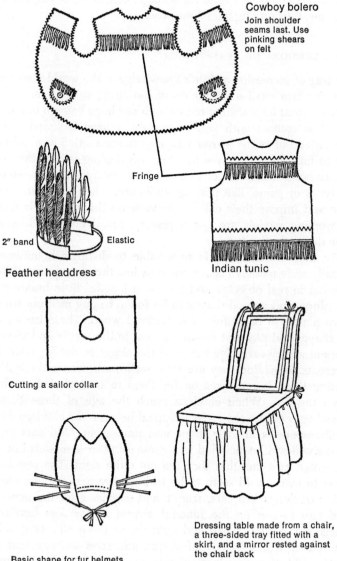

Cowboy bolero
Join shoulder
seams last. Use
pinking shears
on felt

Fringe

2" band   Elastic

Feather headdress

Indian tunic

Cutting a sailor collar

Dressing table made from a chair,
a three-sided tray fitted with a
skirt, and a mirror rested against
the chair back

Basic shape for fur helmets

Fig. 12

to the fun if you have room to store them (see Fig. 12). The orange box could be useful for storage, of course, at the end of the game, thus serving a dual purpose.

SCALE VERSIONS OF REAL THINGS

One way of increasing a child's knowledge of the world about us is to give him small-scale models of buildings, vehicles, animals, and so on that he is neither old enough nor large enough to come into close contact with and appreciate. I have included them here instead of in the learning by experience section as children love to imagine themselves in situations dealing with a fleet of cars, or herd of animals, or in a small-size village. This is one of the types of game, like playing dollhouse, when they can conceive and impose their child's-eye view on things. This is why self-working models are not necessary. Small children like to move things themselves.

One may wonder if it is reasonable to distinguish between virtually scale models (i.e., in more or less the same proportions as found in real objects) and the more fanciful little buildings, cars, ships, and animal shapes to be found in any medium from cheap plastic to beautifully hand-carved wood. These imaginative shapes and pleasant finishes appeal to the tactile and visual senses at a very early age for what the object is, not for what it represents. Providing they are safe, well made, and esthetically pleasing there is every reason for them to be included in the baby's toy box. When children reach the age of three these things begin to lose their visual appeal because the children can see discrepancies in their shape and proportion. Odd cars and wagons will still be included in a game using scale models but it is accepted as a fact that they are not quite right. The sensible course to take would seem to be to buy only reasonably scaled models of things like cars, trucks, and engines after the age of three and to confine the fanciful shapes to the less familiar objects, e.g. a Noah's Ark and animals, or those objects which exist is such a multiplicity of shapes and sizes anyway that a slightly odd though pleasing size may nevertheless be authentic.

Cars, trucks, trains, etc. For vehicles the most that is necessary is wheels that turn and accurate coloring and shaping. Older children are delighted with the new developments shown by their old favorites in the form of luggage compartments and hoods that open, independent suspension, minute bits of fawn plastic supposed to represent luggage, plastic windows, simulated upholstery and steering wheels. This is completely lost on the preschool child who is quite happy just to "brrm, brrm" his way around the floor with a simple but accurate and sturdy shape of a car or truck. Should it be something special such as a crane, dump truck, garbage truck, or other utilitarian vehicle, then it is appreciated if there is a simple way of lifting, dumping, or loading, but the very smallness of size makes anything elaborate frustrating and fragile.

There is a wide range of size, type, and quality available in toy vehicles and most children have examples of various kinds providing them with a rather mixed fleet. There are obvious advantages in having a collection from the same range if this is possible but children don't see anything wrong in using a 3-inch tow truck to tow a 12-inch car if it will work. Indeed through play of this kind they come to realize that progress is most satisfactory when the right-size-for-the-right-job rule is observed. The largest manufacturers of scale vehicle toys are very well known and produce more than adequate catalogs. If money is short a few cents spent on one of these little booklets will entertain small children for a long time.

When buying a wheeled toy choose a simple one without expensive frills which "does" something. Dump trucks and cranes seem to be top favorites with fire engines and bulldozers not far behind. Leave the more elaborate designs and clockwork motors for the older children. Friction-driven motors are suitable for young children but these essentially require freedom to zoom along alone which means the child is not really in control as he likes to be.

Trains are difficult. Baby versions are regarded as just another set of vehicles, but from three onward most children know perfectly well that trains go on tracks. It is wise to delay a windup set until the age of five when the pleasure of switching on and off is appreciated. Pushing vehicles along on a single track is adequate at three. Electric trains and racing cars are strictly for the older child.

If you are short of money or have to provide enough cars for a large number of children on limited capital (e.g. for a playgroup) rummage sales are a good source of secondhand toys. Because of their sturdy nature all cars need is new tires (which can be bought separately but make sure you get the right size) and a lick of paint. Apart from this you really only have to make the need known to be the recipient of as many of these things as you can deal with. Every growing boy has a few cars his mother is pleased to see disappear.

Garages and roadways. There are ways to add interest to the car game. One can provide a garage, traffic layout, or miniature village for these scale models. Most bought garages are made from hardboard and softwood. It is wise to apply to garages the same rules as buying dollhouses, i.e. not too elaborate, not too fragile, and with plenty of scope for physical and mental activity. There should be one feature which enables the children to do more than just park cars, e.g. a lift or ramp, or there seems little point in providing a garage. Making one is easy. Patterns are available or it may be better to design one with your own storage space limitations in mind. A roof which comes off is a good idea because they are usually played with on the floor and access is easier through the top. Most children are content to make a garage or enclosure with building blocks or cut up a cardboard carton and draw parking lines on it with chalk. A hole cut in the top and a cardboard ramp is all that is needed for a roof parking game. My children just park cars in a bulge under the hearth rug or chalk an enclosure on the yard. The attraction is the rearranging of the cars and observing road traffic protocol.

Some toy suppliers stock units which can be laid out to form tracks and roadways. Some are thick building blocks which may just be used in this way, some are hardboard strips marked out specially for the purpose. Another kind consists of an interlocking wooden track incorporating a bridge which teams up with a take-to-pieces ferry boat and train. Yet another has units which clip together. Some are expensive and some are reasonably priced, most are adequate for the strain they will have to take, and all of them add to the game. They all need storing and buying so it is a question of what storage space you can spare and whether you can afford them. All that you are essentially supplying is a defined track along which to push vehicles. This need could equally well be filled by strips of paper or cardboard (about 5 inches wide is a good size), plain strips of hardboard or offcuts of hardboard (see Fig. 13). An intersection (a curved X-shape) is pleasant but one can manage without. A long strip can be raised to make a hill by pushing a brick underneath. Children can mark off their own traffic signs in chalk or crayon and even little children can manage white lines.

Outside traffic play is even easier. Chalk marks on a hard surface or small sticks marking out a road system on grass will give a flexible arrangement that can spread as wide as space allows. This may lead to a problem. If play space is short the road layout has to be limited so that reasonable bounds are kept. Indoors the easiest way to do this is paint or mark a road layout on a sheet of hardboard, cardboard, or strong paper. Obviously hardboard is most serviceable (see Fig. 13). This can be placed on a table or floor but it is best made only just as wide as a child can reach (20 ins. x 40 ins. is a good size). If the space is so generous they have to crawl over the board or paper, it is difficult and distracting, and the whole object of a play board of this kind is to limit space. The roads should go round the circumference, not straight across and off a precipice at the edge. When the outside road has been marked the center may be filled with a maze of roads or contain defined areas which are neutral in appearance so that they can represent parking lots, gravel pits, brick works, circus encampments, or whatever the game happens to demand this time. A play board can be supported on two chair seats facing each other if the edges are strengthened by a batten frame with two extra battens across the width to keep it rigid.

There are several versions of small buildings one can buy. These may be used alone or added to traffic games. The plastic kits which appeal to an eight-year-old are too difficult to make and fragile to use for a younger child. The other types are mainly

Traffic layouts

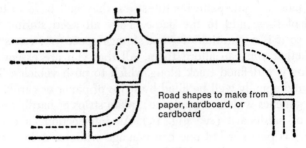

Road shapes to make from paper, hardboard, or cardboard

Traffic board

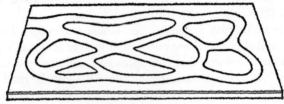

Hardboard sheet edged with batten

Fort

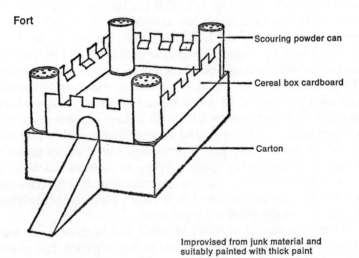

Scouring powder can

Cereal box cardboard

Carton

Improvised from junk material and suitably painted with thick paint

Fig. 13

made of solid wood either quite crudely or beautifully finished and may be bought as sets or units. Naturally the finish affects the price. If you can afford it the smooth polished versions are pleasant to handle but most children are happy to manage without or simulate buildings by placing building blocks in strategic positions. One can improvise by using small cartons and sticky tape. Colored sticky paper is easier to apply than poster paint as most cartons have a slightly waxed finish. Rest assured, if your children demand buildings they will find something from somewhere.

Soldiers and forts. Toy soldiers and forts are not such favorites as they used to be with small boys although the range available for buying is large. Plastic figures are much stronger than the lead ones our grandfathers played with and forts can be large or small, grand or simple depending on how much you are prepared to pay.

Forts can be made quite easily. It is a good idea to use the hollow base as a storage box. The whole superstructure is the lid and is attached by long hinges. For one afternoon's fun scouring powder tin towers fastened to a cardboard carton and castellated cardboard walls are quite good enough (see Fig. 13).

Animals and farm buildings. At the age of three most children know what animals should look like and appreciate the very good, solid plastic models which are reasonably cheap and virtually unbreakable. Games of farmyard, wild beasts, or circus will alternate or mingle with traffic play. One can buy attractive farmyard units, elaborate ranches with fences and corrals, or layouts showing fields or zoo enclosures with the appropriate fences, etc. Most of these items are pleasant and well made but if money is limited it is wiser to buy the animals and make or improvise the rest. The tiny buildings necessary for a farm can be made of hardboard pieces just stuck with impact glue and painted. Their small size and closeknit nature gives the strength they need. They may be decorated with paint where appropriate, but it is better to keep them simple. If storage space is limited, make a kennel to fit into a pigsty which fits into a cowshed which fits into a stable which fits into a house which fits into a barn and so on (see Fig. 14). Cardboard boxes of varying sizes are adequate for an impromptu game.

If your children or space limitations demand a layout rather than a free space, use the same technique as for a traffic layout. Better still, make the farm, zoo, or circus layout on the other side

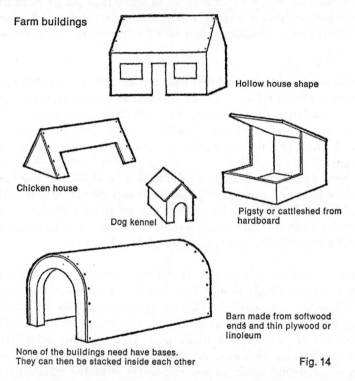

Farm buildings

Hollow house shape

Chicken house

Dog kennel

Pigsty or cattleshed from hardboard

Barn made from softwood ends and thin plywood or linoleum

None of the buildings need have bases.
They can then be stacked inside each other

Fig. 14

of the traffic board and save money and space. If you are really ambitious and clever, make a simple box shape 4 ins. deep x 20 ins. wide by however long you have room for, from 1-inch softwood sides and plywood or hardboard top and bottom. Instead of filling in one long side leave it open to accommodate pull-out trays or drawers made to fit. Keep the necessary toys in these and paint two different layouts on the top and bottom.

Make sure the drawers containing the toys are put in opposite ways as appropriate.

Improvising is fun for farmyards and zoos, as all kinds of interesting materials can be stuck to a sheet of cardboard to represent different textures. Use rice for gravel, sand for earth, green poster paint made thick enough to rough up with a stick (by adding flour or wallpaper-paste powder) for grass, tweed scraps of suitable color and nubby texture for rocks or anything appropriate. Ponds may be represented by cooking foil anchored down by a rim of modeling clay. Make fences from used matchsticks or jackstraws and matchboxes. Shaped objects can be sculpted from modelling clay or dough with a one-third salt to flour recipe. When these materials dry out they can be painted—even varnished if you get carried away.

I hope you and the children do get carried away. That is the aim of imaginative play and it can happen even if you have little or no money. If you stick to improvised things which can be thrown away you can even manage without storage space.

6

Adventure Play

A SENSE OF ADVENTURE can result from overcoming unfamiliar obstacles or experiencing strange sensations. As our environment becomes safer, more stereotyped, and, for small children, more restricted, there are fewer natural physical obstacles although the mental ones certainly don't get any less. Children develop the ability to face and overcome difficulties (courage, if you like) at an early age if only we give them the chance. Naturally it is better if they practice on smaller, less important hurdles first. True country living is ideal from this point of view. There are trees to climb, gates to scramble over, woods to play hide-and-seek in, brooks with stepping-stones to balance on, humpy ground to slide down or roll on, and strange paths to follow. The number of children living in such rural conditions is not large. Country villages are urbanizing at an alarming rate and in some country towns without adequate parks or play space the children are farther from a large open area than their fellows living in the center of the city. With a little ingenuity and help it should be possible to emulate, if not improve on, natural hazards.

CLIMBING MATERIAL

The use and object of climbing material is obvious. Muscles develop, balance improves, and self-confidence increases. If you have a tree in your back yard then you are well equipped. If not you can buy, make, or improvise a climbing unit.

To buy. If you have money and space, all the big toy firms can provide you with a climbing frame. Some are of wood, some of tubular metal, some can have other bits added such as a plank to form a slide, some have features such as doors which enable them to be used for outside house play. They are similar in shape and construction but vary slightly in price and size as one would expect. I have heard praise for most kinds and blame for most kinds. You must decide whether metal will be more durable than wood but less pleasant to touch. If you have money but are not so happily placed for play space (these things are difficult to take down for storage) there are other ways of buying climbing apparatus.

A hexagonal or dome shape may suit your space better or a unit of the five-bar-gate type supported by heavy, wide feet at each end. This is narrower than a square frame (see Fig. 15). Another style is a horizontal ladder supported 5 feet or so from the ground by ladders at each end, each of which is fastened to a very solid, wide foot. These are available in wood and metal, don't take much room, can be moved about, and can be used indoors if the playroom is big enough (see Fig. 16).

Yet another type of climbing unit is a trestle shape—rather like a stepladder with steps on both sides. Some fold or adjust and may be metal or wood. These may be used alone or in conjunction with cleated planks to form a slide, bridge, or sort of cat-walk. If the trestle is small enough it can be used as the pivot for a seesaw (see Fig. 16). Some of these trestle-shaped units come with wheels fixed on and a steering unit (they are called Vari-play Triangle sets) and can be used in many different ways alone or with other units. You will have to pay between sixty and two hundred and fifty dollars, depending on what you choose, so time and thought spent on measuring up and looking at what is available is a good investment. If it is imperative to remove the climbing apparatus at the end of each session, climbing nets are a useful type though expensive and heavy to handle. These are very strong rope nets which fix over a permanent frame and are securely fastened to it. When space is virtually nonexistent horizontal bars on tubular metal supports are reasonably cheap and provide something to swing on like a monkey if not climb. Just a ladder is better than nothing.

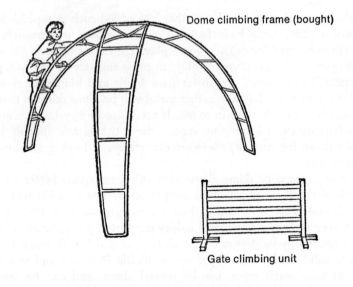

Dome climbing frame (bought)

Gate climbing unit

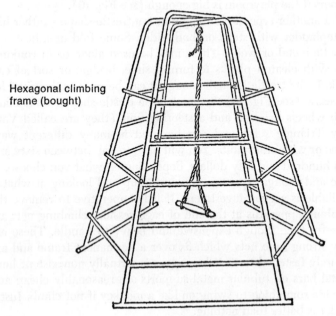

Hexagonal climbing frame (bought)

Fig. 15

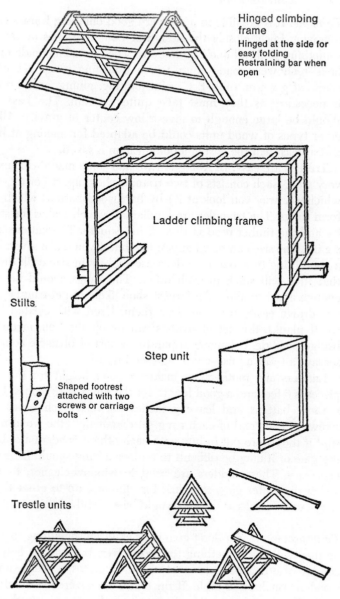

Hinged climbing frame
Hinged at the side for easy folding
Restraining bar when open

Ladder climbing frame

Stilts

Shaped footrest attached with two screws or carriage bolts

Step unit

Trestle units

Fig. 16

To make. It is possible to make very good climbing frames either following fairly closely the design of bought frames or creating something to fit all one's limitations. The best homemade ones I have seen were made from 1-inch doweling rungs set into a frame of 3 x 3-in. timber. Careful jointing, gluing, and screwing is necessary as they must take quite a strain. The base area should be large enough to give a low center of gravity. All the other types of wood units could be adapted for making at home and at least half the cost of a bought item is saved.

Trestles are easy. In Abingdon we had some made which work very well. Each consists of two triangles held apart (or together, whichever way you look at it) by hardwood battens which thus form rungs. The triangles are equilateral which makes for stability and the timber used is 1½ x 1½ ins. square. The battens are 1 x 2 ins. The size can be what you like but if you make several it is a good thing to make them decrease slightly in size each time so that they will stack in each other. The rungs should be wide enough apart to allow the largest shoe likely to get caught to be withdrawn easily from between them. Used with cleated hardwood planks, this set of trestles can be climbed on, made into bridges, a slide, balancing apparatus, a sort of obstacle course, a seesaw, a train, a bus—anything (see Fig. 16).

Ladders any mother can make. A good height for the side-pieces is 6 feet and a good length for the rungs is 18 inches. Use 2 x 1½-in. battens and leave 9 inches between each rung. Two screws at each end of each rung set diagonally (the wood might split if they were put in line with each other) is adequate. Don't use glue or it may be difficult to replace a rung should it become necessary. These ladders are used in window-cleaner, fireman, and wall-painter games, or just for climbing up to other things. Large metal hooks at the end would be a useful addition.

To improvise. If you don't give your children something to climb on they will find something for themselves. It might be better to compromise and provide a set of sturdy crates, a plank, an old wooden armchair, or table. If the crates are covered with leftover paint they look better, of course. The only essential is that the material should be reasonably safe and splinter- or nail-free.

Hammering nails in firmly can be done by the children with a little supervision.

Climbing indoors. Indoor provision in a large playroom is easier than a normal home. Boxes, small trestles, and very old furniture given up for the purpose will do if you can't manage the larger climbing apparatus. I find it best to restrict a "just climbing" game to the hall but usually it is part of another game, which may make things difficult. If you can't stand the noise and there isn't a park it might be better to find a suitable fence or gate along your shopping route and turn a blind eye.

BALANCING MATERIAL

All climbing material provides scope for developing muscle control and coordination which leads to good balance. There is some material made specifically for balancing practice. Quite often small children find balancing just on their feet more difficult than climbing with feet and hands together.

To buy. Most of the large toy manufacturers produce a balancing rail. Some are beams which can be supported in specially shaped supports. Some provide two different heights by varying the supports. One firm produces narrow balancing boards which fix on to blocklike wooden supports with a doweling peg to keep them fixed. Another firm produces a parallel bar unit to be used with trestle climbing frames as supports. This type enables the children to place both feet naturally instead of one in front of the other.

Educational firms provide gymnasium benches which have a narrow beam on their bottom surface; thus when turned upside down they become very solid balancing rails. If you can afford it this might be a most useful piece of equipment serving a dual purpose.

Walking, or learning to walk, on stilts is another way of developing good balance. Make sure they are well made and that the footrest is double-bolted to the upright otherwise it could swivel round as it becomes loose.

A pogo stick is another balance toy which children enjoy once they can jump on it but makes them furious until they do manage. Unfortunately the good ones are rather expensive.

To make. One can make balance rails quite quickly from a piece of 3 x 4-in. timber lodged into shaped supports. A narrow plank (of hardwood) with cleats at each end could be used, placed on the lowest rung of trestle supports or put across a sandpit. As the children get more confident they will put it higher. These balancing rails are necessarily narrow and one must ensure that they are placed firmly or they may tip under pressure. No great damage is likely to ensue as they should never be too high, but it might put off a child who is just starting to make progress.

Stilts too are easy to make at home. Hardwood is best but softwood stands up to wear and tear quite adequately. Use 2 x 1-in. battens for the uprights and make them as high, or just a bit less, than the child who is going to use them. The footrest is made from a piece of 2 x 3-in. timber 6 inches long. Shape it by cutting off a wedge starting halfway down the 6-inch side so that the 3-inch measurement is whittled down to a ½-inch. Drill two holes in this narrowing piece large enough to take a substantial carriage bolt. Make corresponding holes in the uprights starting 6 inches or 9 inches from the ground (see Fig. 16). More holes can be made as the child grows. Bolt on the footrest and all that remains is to shape a handrest by beveling the corners and sandpapering. For a very small child it might be necessary to screw a little platform to the top surface of the footrest to give more space for his foot to rest on. A piece of 3 x 6 x ½-in. wood should be adequate.

To improvise. Most children find walking along a curb quite enough practice in balancing but this may not be possible in a busy street. Ordinary bricks laid end to end or curbstones would be very much appreciated in a garden (by the children). A galvanized iron pipe set securely in supports would do. Some flat stones set into the lawn could look quite pleasing and make a useful jumping course. Flat slices from a large tree trunk serve the same purpose. If this is impossible then everyone can manage a bit of chalk to make "stepping-stones" on the driveway. A series of old car tires laid flat is fun to walk on or jump along. The children will find something even if it's only hopping along the squared linoleum in the kitchen.

Improvised stilts made from tin cans are great fun. You need a pair of strong cans with proper lids. Thread a long piece of sturdy string through holes bored in the can opposite each other and just under the top edge. Stand the child on the cans and tie the string with a long loop so that he can just hold it comfortably. He should then be able to walk along, keeping the can touching his foot by means of lifting the loops as he lifts his feet. (These are not recommended for use on a polished floor, of course.)

PHYSICAL ACTION MATERIAL

There are some toys which encourage muscular development but their main attraction for children is that they can go up and down or whiz around fast or indulge in some other stomach-jolting movement not ordinarily possible. We may provide them because they encourage physical activity, provide another "fear" obstacle to overcome, or just because they are fun. One can buy, make, improvise, or even borrow these items as most children's playgrounds have swings, a seesaw, and a chute or those delightful tumble tubs. In fact the equipment found in parks is larger and stronger than one can provide or accommodate for a playgroup or home, so it may be more sensible to rely on a public playground if there is one fairly near.

Swings. If you have to buy a swing you will find that they are the most reasonably priced toys available, but a careful inspection before buying pays dividends. Some rest on the ground, some can be anchored. They should all have a reasonably low center of gravity when the child is at the highest possible position; thus a wide base is necessary. The main objection to them is their "one-at-a-time" aspect. It is asking for trouble to have a queue near a swinging child and to have two on one swing doesn't solve the problem. If you have more than one child to provide for, you can buy wider frames with two swings. A better idea is a wide frame fitted with a "tire" seat, hand loops, and a rope ladder or climbing net either together or one at a time (see Fig. 17). This way the equipment is more versatile and less lethal. It is the heavy, high-swinging seat types that do the damage.

If you have a suitable tree then just a rope (looped to provide a foothold) slung from a bough is fine. Very little children would perhaps be better off with an enclosed chair seat. Light children can swing in a doorway if you have no space and are willing to make holes above the lintel to thread ropes through, but this needs a careful warning system. Swing frames can be made from hardwood timber or 4-inch poles. They must be adequately anchored and weatherproofed. Just sticking them into the ground is not enough. Tubular metal is another suitable material. The ground beneath swings can become muddy and unpleasant but a concrete base is terribly dangerous to the heads and limbs of falling children. Hardening the ground with ashes is a good compromise.

Slides. These are another playground favorite. Good safe ones are expensive to buy and if they are not safe are expensive at any price. Storage space may limit the size but apart from this it is worth buying the tallest version you can afford. Every slide should have a hand grip for the top step and, since children don't attempt any apparatus until they can manage it, a large slide is quite safe even for the youngest users. If they are used indoors on a polished surface rubber grips are necessary to prevent skidding. Very few small slides have the end of the chute raised from the ground, so an old rug is useful to prevent bottoms being grazed on concrete or grass.

Slides can be made from hardwood, hardboard, and doweling rungs but improvisation is easier. A polished plank hooked on to other apparatus is adequate—a strong stepladder will serve the purpose. A plank and a box will do or perhaps your back yard or garden has a raised surface or low wall you could use. These dodges have the advantage of helping with the storage problem. The rule should be: the higher they are the safer they must be, but let the children experiment. They are usually very careful.

Homemade rocker

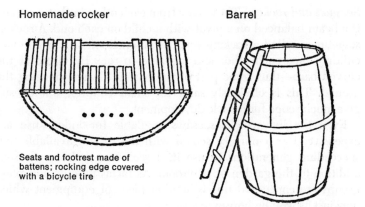

Seats and footrest made of
battens; rocking edge covered
with a bicycle tire

Barrel

Provide a ladder for climbing in

Go-cart

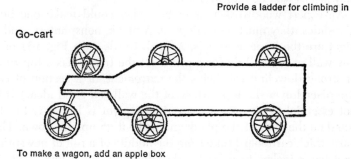

To make a wagon, add an apple box

**Homemade
swing unit**

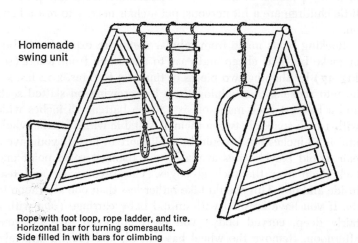

Rope with foot loop, rope ladder, and tire.
Horizontal bar for turning somersaults.
Side filled in with bars for climbing

Fig. 17

Seesaws and rockers. These vary from each other in that a seesaw is a beam balanced on a pivot with a child on each end. A rocker, sometimes called a rocking boat, is an enclosed seat where two children face each other and are able to rock by virtue of the curved base—thus some part of the base is always touching the ground. This is obviously safer for small children but doesn't give much scope for muscle development.

Even the lightweight seesaws available for indoor use are expensive. For a nursery school with the capital available and succeeding generations to use it, a seesaw may be a pleasant addition to the garden or playroom. As far as parents and play-groups are concerned this is another piece of equipment which may just as well be improvised or made.

An expert woodworker or metalworker could make one but, like slides, they must be made safe. A plank, nonsplintery, and a pivot are the basic essentials. A small trestle (see Fig. 16) or a low wall or log will do for a pivot. (If the trestle has a top rung of strong doweling this helps the movement, or a section of car tire placed over the top surface of the wall is a good idea.) It is not essential to sit on a seesaw. If the pivot is low it is fun to stand on the ends of the plank and make it go up and down. The hard, thick cardboard tube from the middle of a roll of newsprint or a log 4 inches in diameter do admirably for a low pivot. If little children are a bit nervous, put a chair nearby to rest a hand on.

Rocking boats made from tubular metal are expensive to buy or make but it is cheap and easy to make one from wood (see Fig. 17) by shaping two pieces of timber 3 ft. 6 ins. x 12 ins. x 1 in. into rockers, then joining them by screwing on slatted seats and a footrest each made of six 18-inch battens 1½ inches wide with 1-inch spaces between them. A suitable width for the whole unit is 18 inches but it could be a bit more or less. If you have a pair of old bicycle tires available, cut them at some point and tack them over the rocking edges. This saves wear and tear inside and out. This should take rather less than one afternoon to do. If you have finished with an old baby carriage (one with a fairly deep, curved body) you need not even give up your afternoon. Remove the wheel base, hood, and handle and take out the center section of the mattress support to allow space for feet. There you have a good solid rocker. The wheels can be used to make a wagon, the hood can be hammered on to an orange-box sports car, and the handle will come in for a homemade vehicle of some kind.

Rocking horses are a "one-at-a-time" version of a rocker. A properly shaped horse of a fair size will cost you around eighty dollars. There are small versions obtainable and if your child desperately desires one they might be worth considering. Regarded purely as a toy, they leave little scope for action and if a child is playing make-believe "horsy" games, he is probably more than willing to imagine the horse too.

Trampolines. A trampoline is a sprung canvas sheet which enables one to jump to a great height and do acrobatics meanwhile. Gymnastically speaking it gives a short time in a weightless state between landings. Children would certainly enjoy one and it would provide jumping exercise but any wider benefit than that is doubtful. If you should have an old spring mattress which they can jump, roll, and somersault on, that is fine.

WHEELED VEHICLES

There are many kinds of vehicles which provide scope for muscular activity especially to legs and feet: bicycles, tricycles, pedal cars, go-carts, scooters, wagons. Perhaps sleds should be included here although they are somewhat different in character.

Tricycles and bicycles. A tricycle is the one thing a child really gets the money's worth from if there is space enough to use it freely. They are safe, easy to propel, and good for exercising feet and legs. By three most children have outgrown their small one and want a big one. If you fancy horns, leather seats, and front baskets, in other words a deluxe version, you will have to pay a lot. For a plain serviceable type you might get away with about twenty-five dollars for a new one. Tricycles are so strong that a secondhand one is a good idea. New wheels, hand grips, pedals, chains, etc., can be provided if necessary and a coat of paint soon makes them new-looking enough for a three-year-old. The obvious advantages of solid tires outweigh the slight discomfort.

Another course you might take is to miss the big tricycle stage and go straight on to a very small bicycle with stabilizers. Children must be able to put both their feet on the ground when learning to ride a bicycle so their first one must be small at whatever age they have it. It may seem wasteful to buy one which will be outgrown in a year or two, especially if there is no one to hand it on to, but it is far better to keep the child safe by buying the next size and selling the outgrown one. There are some bicycles on the market which allow for leg growth by having an adjustable saddle position. For a very small child it is again better to have solid tires if you can get them. Brakes must be strong and carefully maintained. This will preserve shoe toes as well as prevent accidents. Little boys do love to have cross bars but this is not safe for learning to ride. Another point worth mentioning is that the safety of other people depends on your child's road sense. Do lay down family rules to suit the laws of your locality about how and where and when to ride. Spend some time on formal training in safety rules—many states have laws regulating bicycles.

Pedal cars and scooters. One child may love his pedal car, another child may completely ignore exactly the same model. The prices vary from just possible to frankly ridiculous depending on which version you choose. Obviously one should inspect carefully before buying, paying particular attention to how the wheels are fixed on and whether the pedaling mechanism is made in heavy-duty material and is the right size. Scooters are cheaper than cars and provide a slightly different type of muscular exercise but not many children manage them well. They do not have the same mechanical efficiency as a tricycle and children subconsciously realize this. If you can afford or have room for only one item, bicycles or tricycles are the best buy. Bicycles, tricycles, cars, and scooters are not an asset for a playgroup. They go too fast and are "one-at-a-time" toys. Far better spend the money and space on something else. Children can play with their own tricycles at home.

Go-carts and wagons. Go-carts and wagons either bought or homemade are fun for home and playgroup use. Some go-carts are hand propelled which is good for the arm muscles. Others are just a long seat on a wheel base which one paddles along with arms and feet. They are easy to make or improvise from sets of stroller or baby carriage wheels or even from the raw materials (see Fig. 17). Wheels may be bought from hardware or toy shops and a metal dealer will sell you steel rod for axles or make them up if you describe what you need. A box or plank on top makes the wagon bed. To steer it a set of front wheels mounted on a beam swiveled on a carriage bolt fitting is adequate. If there is a big brother of ten-plus around, the whole affair can be left to him to improvise.

Another good idea is to add wheels to a wooden sled, thus doubling its useful life. A simple sled can be made in one afternoon from runners shaped from a piece of 1 x 9-in. timber in any length you wish (try 3 feet). Curve the front edge of the runners and use battens to make a slatted seat. A strengthening batten stuck along the top inner edge of each runner is a good idea. Metal strip screwed on to the business edge of the runners will protect them and improve performance.

MATERIAL WHICH COMBINES ADVENTURE
AND IMAGINATIVE PLAY

Children do not climb for the sake of exercising muscles. They do all these active things because they enjoy the sensation, want to overcome an obstacle, or as part of another game. There is some equipment which provides scope for muscular activity and imaginative games at the same time: such as large barrels, concrete pipes, a stack of crates, or old car tires which can be moved, jumped on, sat in, built with, crawled through, or anything else you can think of. All these things add greatly to the attraction of outdoor play and need not cost anything. Some nursery schools and parks are lucky enough to have an old car or road roller (carefully anchored of course) which is delightful. A large barrel could be a helicopter, submarine, elevator, or bus one day, and, with adequate supervision, the next day can be pro-

98 *Adventure Play*

pelled around the yard by means of a crawling movement inside
it. Some kind of dolly enables children to move a huge stack of
boxes or crates around for many undefined purposes. A pile of
car tires can be a well, a set of stepping-stones . . . all we have to
think about is how to provide them. The children will do the rest.

TRANSPORTATION TOYS

Toys such as wheelbarrows, wagons, trucks, and porters' dollies
are difficult to place because they come into so many kinds of
play—adventure, imaginative, creative, etc. However, you will
find the range of things available to buy is very wide, on the
whole good, and, compared with some other categories, reasonably priced. You should find something to suit you but do check
construction and, for a young child, have an adequate number of
wheels. One-wheel things are difficult to manage. If you can buy
a versatile object like a wagon so much the better. If storage is a
problem a porter's dolly is suitably thin. All these things can be
made and improvised—a set of wheels and a support or container are basic. After that one can elaborate as desired.

There are one or two problems connected with such material,
mainly storage. If there is a covered outside space, this is fine. If
not, a tarpaulin or low shed may be the answer. One must work
out the best method of stacking and make sure whoever is to do
the packing away is aware of the procedure. It might be worth
saving for one of those rather gay canopy arrangements, intended for motorcycles and cars, which can be attached to a
wall. Naturally this is not so important for one's own home as for
a playgroup using other people's premises.

INDOOR PROVISION

It is scope for adventure play that the housebound, yardless child
lacks most of all. Most of the equipment is too large and expensive for a family to provide. The best solution is to find a
playgroup or park but, failing that, one must find small items
which give opportunity for the same kind of exercise. A large
solid train or truck which can be sat on and propelled with the

feet is good or a strong wooden benchtype stool with casters on would do. A rocking boat or rocking horse could be a substitute for a seesaw. It is possible to buy a set of three steps which is essentially a hollow unit (see Fig. 16). This may be walked up, jumped from, sat on, or crawled through when placed on its side. An ordinary set of steps, a short ladder, or a set of crates provide climbing exercise. A trestle-type climbing frame hinged at the top so that it folds flat may not be out of the question (see Fig. 16).

If even these ideas are impossible, you will just have to adopt a more liberal attitude to playing on the stairs. Children who are not allowed to develop at the right age will never have the same inner drive to do so later. We might as well let nature work for us as thwart it.

7

Creative Play

CREATING, experimenting, and learning go hand in hand. This results in a closer understanding and increasing skill as time goes by. All the natural materials mentioned in Chapter 3 are used for creative play but are altered in shape and consistency rather than composition. There comes a time when children are ready to mix paint and paper and make a drawing, to make a scrapbook, or do other irreversible things. Creative play may be undertaken for its own sake or as a natural adjunct to other activities. Its value is self-evident. Opportunity for imagination, skill, and learning are particularly important because once a child reaches school age he has to learn with many other children at a similar pace. Thus opportunities for free imaginative and creative play are necessarily limited to allow time for more academic learning. Wide provision for creative play should be made in the home at all ages. Fortunately it doesn't cost much money and the equipment need not be elaborate.

PAINTING

Most people think of painting as something one must do with a brush. The basic essentials are coloring matter and somewhere to apply it. Bright yellow mud thrown on a wall will do if nothing else is available.

Paint and brushes. There are one or two rules to observe when buying paint and brushes for picture painting. The smaller the child the bigger the brush and the thicker the paint should be. A three-year-old would enjoy a 2-inch paint brush or even a larger

size. Fine artists' brushes should be kept for much older children.
Even an eight-year-old likes a ½-inch brush to use in conjunction with finer ones. Paint which can be directly applied is easier
than cakes or tubes. Thus poster or powder paint is the best buy.
One can add wallpaper-paste powder to thicken powder paint.
This is very convenient as it prevents drips and the children can
apply a satisfying daub with each stroke. As only primary colors
and black and white need be bought, this is just as cheap as
those huge, rather unpleasant paintboxes most children are given
at one time or another. For a large number of children, it is more
economical to mix a week's supply of paint at a time and keep it
in screw-top jars or the plastic bottles detergents come in. One
can then put out enough for one day at a time in plastic glasses.
Deep containers are less likely to splash than shallow ones. For
one child one can mix the primary colors in jars and then allow
daily mixing for the greens, browns, grays, and pinks. Black and
white are important for use alone or to make varying shades of
color. If you have enough capital to buy the large tins of powder
paint or could share with a neighbor or another group, this is
much cheaper than buying small quantities.

Encourage children to take one color at a time from a central
tray and return it before they take another. In this way one can
leave the brush in the pot and the colors remain clear instead of
becoming more khaki as the painting progresses. This is also
more economical as one need only provide one jar of each color.
For the child who has only one brush, teach him to rinse the
brush in a water jar before going on to the next color.

Special paint-wiping cloths hung on the easel will soon be
used automatically where necessary, but if the floor is precious a
sheet or two of newspaper may be useful for placing beneath the
easel.

Another brush and paint activity is finishing off aeroplanes or
daggers made at the carpenter's bench or just brightening up
orange boxes or crates. Large brushes and leftover bits of primer
paint are useful here. Adequate protection all round is essential
as this kind of paint will not wash out or off when dry. For
impromptu games a bucket of water and a whitewash brush are
fine for painting walls.

If you have no brushes or just feel like a change, finger painting and blob painting are fun. Finger painting, good thick paint (it may be bought specially or just be ordinary, well-thickened poster paint) applied with the fingers—arms and elbows too probably—on to a slightly waxed surface, is very satisfying to do. Use a piece of cardboard from a waxy carton or paper rubbed lightly with a piece of candle. The effect can be varied by using a comb or fork to make striated patterns. Blob painting is done by putting blobs of thickish paint on to a sheet of paper and folding it into two or four so that the marks are transferred from one side to the other. If the paper is cut into some shape first such as a butterfly or flower the result can be quite pleasing.

It is possible to apply paint with a piece of potato or carrot either just cut across or carved to give a simple shape. Another pattern "applier" can be made by sticking a piece of cord or rope in an interesting coil or shape on to a flat piece of wood with household cement (see Fig. 19). This raised pattern is dipped in thin paint (on a plate or tray is best) and applied to paper or fabric. A simple handle on the piece of wood makes the whole process much easier. Think before saying "No" to a suggestion. If you stop to consider properly you may find that the children have come up with a good idea of their own.

Paper. The need for paper is inevitable at some stage. Once you have realized that children paint for fun and neither want nor appreciate their work being taken too seriously, the need for expensive paper disappears. A small piece of paper is no good to a young child. Newsprint is large, absorbent, freely available and more than adequate. Leftover wallpaper can be used for painting on the wrong side and has other uses for its right side, so never throw it away. Most newspaper offices will give you or sell you for very little the end bit of one of those huge rolls of newsprint. They may be 6 feet wide and 18 inches in diameter so make sure of transportation first. This roll can be sawed into two or three narrower rolls and lengths cut off as necessary. A printing firm may be a good source of offcuts of paper but the pieces are usually small. Ask your local butcher where he gets his wrapping paper rolls from and he may offer to include one for you in his next order. In other words—be paper-minded and you should have no difficulty at all.

Easels, etc. We now have paper, brushes, and paint. The next thing is where to rest the paper. The obvious place is a low table or floor, but horizontal painting may present smudging difficulties. It is certainly easier to paint a good big picture when the paper is nearly vertical. If the paint is adequately thickened, drips and runs should not be a problem. It is possible to buy free-standing easels made of wood or tubular metal. Some provide space for two children facing each other; one type even has a triangular shape thus accommodating three children. Some fold, some do not, so your storage facilities may affect which you buy. Most have a tray to hold paint jars which is very useful. A table easel consisting of two inclined surfaces hinged at their top edge and having a cord or chain limiting how far their bottom edges can be placed apart is available from several firms. I would never advise a one-sided, old-fashioned easel. They do not stand well and have space for only one child or activity. If you only need to provide space for one child, you could have a double easel with a painting board on one side and a blackboard on the other. To buy easels will cost between three and fifteen dollars depending on the model you choose.

For the expenditure of about two dollars and a couple of hours (allowing drying time for impact glue) one can make a perfectly satisfactory double easel. All it consists of is two pieces of hardboard or plywood (2 feet square is a useful size) framed with 2 x 1-in. battens. Sticking with glue and hardboard nails is enough. The battens should be jointed or fastened with corrugated fasteners. The side battens project downward to form legs. The batten along the top edge is set 2 inches down so that there is space for clothespins to fasten paper on with. The batten along the bottom edge is glued touching the edge and a simple tray for paint jars is screwed to it through the hardboard or plywood. The two sides are fastened together at the top by screwing ordinary hinges to the leg battens. The distance it can open is fixed by attaching a piece of rope or chain to opposite legs (see

Easels

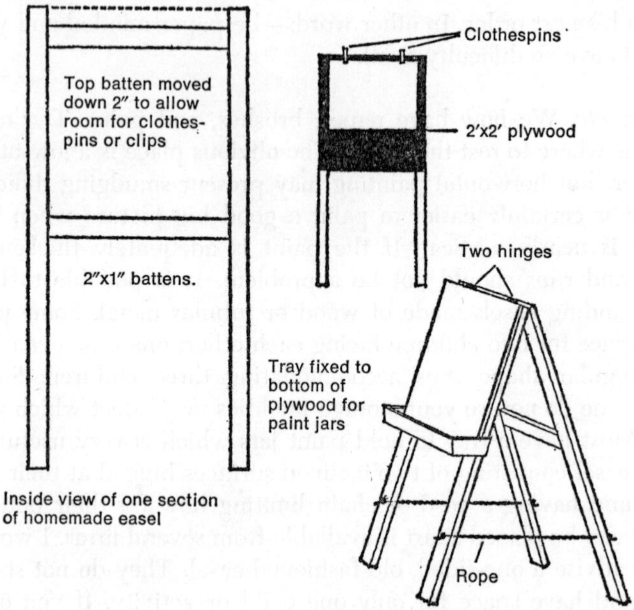

Top batten moved down 2" to allow room for clothespins or clips

2"x1" battens.

Inside view of one section of homemade easel

Clothespins

2'x2' plywood

Two hinges

Tray fixed to bottom of plywood for paint jars

Rope

Blackboards

Three-leaved board fixed to wall

Wider hinges used on side which has to fold on top

Back of leaf which folds on top papered or painted to match wall

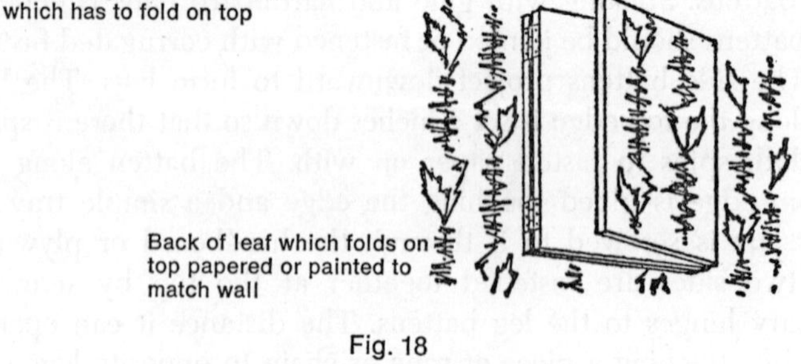

Fig. 18

Fig. 18). A similar arrangement for use on a table can be made without the leg projections.

If you have to improvise, just pinning a sheet of paper to a plain door or wall surface will suffice. Alternatively a piece of any material stiff enough to stand alone (e.g. hardboard, stiff cardboard, plasterboard) can be stood on a chair seat, leaning against the chair back, and have a piece of paper thumbtacked to it. The seat can then be used for a paint shelf but obviously it is wise to protect it with newspaper first.

PENCILS, CRAYONS, CHALKS, ETC.

The same rules apply to these as to paintbrushes. Small children get on better with thicker varieties and it is possible to buy chalks and wax crayons in large sizes. Pencil-type crayons are appreciated by some four-year-olds and over, but small children use them so fiercely that the points are always either broken or worn down. Sharpening them with a pencil sharpener is fun and good for finger exercise but it gets a bit expensive. Pastel crayons are best left till later for the same reason. Fairly new on the market are washable felt-tipped pens. These, on balance, are slightly less messy than chalk and results are pleasanter than those obtained from wax crayons. They are relatively expensive to replace so lavish use is not to be encouraged.

Chalk needs a slightly rough surface to work properly and blackboards are best. One can have fixed blackboards or free-standing ones. The ideal is a long, child-height board painted with blackboard paint, and fixed to a wall so that several children can draw at one time and collaborate on a mural if the urge takes them. If this is inconvenient, a possibility is to attach to the wall a three-leaf blackboard hinged so that the outer two leaves can be folded in to cover the middle one, with the layer which is on top when it is closed decorated to match the rest of the room. This won't make it disappear but does camouflage it (see Fig. 18). One can also have several leaves extending by means of runners, i.e. a sliding-door effect so that it can be reduced to at least half-size at the end of the game. Try these in your hall at home if you don't have carriage, stroller, tricycle, and boots living there already. An easel may be painted with blackboard paint so that it serves for painting and chalking. Heavy, slightly rough paper will do for chalk if you can't make a blackboard. But I would not advise buying one. They are so cheap and easy to make that it is better to use the money to buy those large boxes of chalk which are so much more economical than small ones. You can buy a dustless variety which, though not perfect in this respect, is better than the ordinary kind. Chalking outside is simple. Use the pavement or the wall and have another good game washing it off.

MURALS AND COLLECTIVE EFFORTS

Small children really prefer to be left alone to draw their own version of whatever it is and only ask a bit of praise at the end. Adults should avoid passing on their own preconceived ideas (which are not necessarily good after all) or providing a shape to fill in. Another danger from interfering adults is that of setting a standard which is too high, thus making children dissatisfied with their own efforts. Children may see shapes quite differently from us and should be free to do what they think is right— otherwise how can they develop? However, bearing all these words of warning in mind, there comes a time when a group of children enjoy making a composite effort. If a mural is done in chalk it is easy for the child to rub his bit out and start again if necessary, so it can be done right on the blackboard. Altering paint or crayon is not as easy, so it is a good idea for each child to do his bit separately and cut it out to stick on to the main picture afterward. In this way one can have street scenes, beach scenes, trees loaded with fruit or pretty birds and butterflies, and so on, with each child doing one item and getting a quick result. One can do this with only one child by letting him add a bit when he feels like it. Don't be too ambitious or he will get bored before it is finished.

PAPER PLAY

Paper as a color source. Many people think only of paint and crayon when considering colors, but paper is a source of both

Making patterns

Potato cut in half and shape
carved on the surface

Rope or string stuck to
wooden base with a handle

Designs made of paper

Colored paper units of
same size

Negative   Positive

Shape cut from paper unit

For young children

Negative applied

Positive applied

Background paper marked
off in units

For older children

Basic units cut down
middle and negative and
positive parts used in halves

Collective efforts

Fishes cut from magazines or sticky paper
or drawn on

Background of blue paper

Fig. 19

color and texture variation. Children enjoy cutting shapes from colored sticky paper instead of painting them, or some will play happily with the shapes of colored sticky paper one can buy. You can use colored construction paper and ordinary paper to paste it on. For instance some wallpapers would make a good garden path or wall on a house picture, brown paper would make a field, dark blue paper could be used for a night scene with stars cut from silver paper.

A full-blown effort of this kind, called a collage, is a possible activity for over-fives using cloth, granular material (such as rice, gravel, dried peas or beans, anything in fact, depending on the texture needed) set in plaster of paris or dough or clay plaques. Under-fives are happy to cut shapes from catalogs or Christmas cards and combine these to make a picture or scrapbook.

Simple designs made from colored paper are easy and effective (see Fig. 19). Use ordinary paper for a background and mark it into square or rectangular units. Cut a number of similar sized units in colored paper (gummed or to be pasted on afterward). Cut a simple shape from the colored units, e.g. a tree, soldier, flower. Apply the colored shape to one unit of the background paper and the piece that is left of the colored unit to the next part of the background paper. Carry on filling alternate squares either with a "positive" or "negative" shape. The results are surprisingly good.

A more sophisticated version is to make the colored units and cut out the shape but cut the whole lot down the middle. Half the positive shape is placed in a background unit and the mirror-image negative part is put next to it. The next background unit is filled in similarly with the opposite bits—very attractive and easier to do than explain (see Fig. 19).

Paper as a construction material. Most people know and admire the art of Origami by which paper is folded so that it forms intricate shapes of surprising strength. All that the majority of us can achieve is a paper hat or boat, depending on whether you wear it or sail it, so we have to work out how to make things by cutting and gluing (see Fig. 20). There is the technique of cutting out the flat picture of what you need and making it stand

Paper buildings

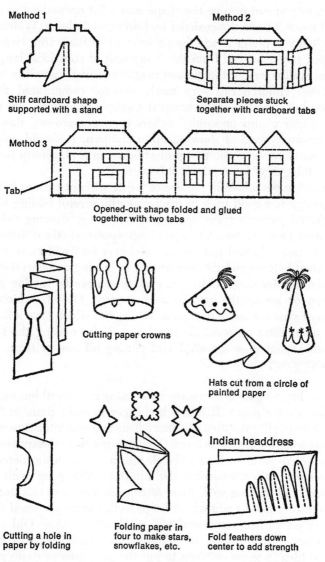

Method 1

Stiff cardboard shape supported with a stand

Method 2

Separate pieces stuck together with cardboard tabs

Method 3

Tab

Opened-out shape folded and glued together with two tabs

Cutting paper crowns

Hats cut from a circle of painted paper

Cutting a hole in paper by folding

Folding paper in four to make stars, snowflakes, etc.

Indian headdress

Fold feathers down center to add strength

Fig. 20

by means of a paper support; or you can cut out pieces and join them with projecting tabs thus getting a three-dimensional effect; or you can resolve the shape into a flat opened-out version and make it three-dimensional by folding and gluing. Whichever method you prefer to use the paper must be fairly stiff. Drawing paper, paper begged from the X-ray unit of your local hospital, some wallpapers, or the glossier magazine covers can all be used.

Small children can very rarely manage complicated things alone but once they have grasped a simple procedure, e.g. making paper chains or sailors' collars or paper crowns, they are surprisingly good at showing other children. It should only be necessary to show one group of children in a playgroup how to do a thing or where equipment is kept.

How to get a hole in a piece of paper without cutting in from the edge is a good trick to teach, how by careful folding to get repeated patterns from one set of holes, e.g. dancing dolls, is another (see Fig. 20). Make sure they appreciate the difference a concertina fold and just an over-and-over fold will make to the finished pattern and the importance of leaving a connecting bit. Symmetry for single objects is easy to achieve by folding paper down or across the middle as necessary. Objects which are almost symmetrical, e.g. cups or kettles, but which have a handle or spout extra on one side can be made by making the shape double-spouted or -handled and cutting off one of them after opening out.

Glue. Proper glue is necessary for sticking cardboard but paste is adequate for paper. It is much cheaper to make paste at home even in small quantities. Ordinary flour and water mixture works quite well, but my favorite method is to put two tablespoons of a powdered paste such as Polycell into a clean plastic detergent container (after removing the squirter), filling up with cold water, and shaking well. After fifteen minutes or so this thickens into a very good paste which keeps well, can be squeezed into a paste jar as necessary, and will wash off clothing. Old toothbrushes, well sterilized, are admirable for applying paste. It is a good idea to teach children to put the glue tube or paste pot in the top of a box or in a saucer. This avoids messy spills.

Transparent tape is useful but brown gummed paper strip is stronger and cheaper for most purposes.

Scissors. With reasonable precautions all children are safe with scissors. Choose the round-ended variety and buy a good quality, otherwise the combination of awkward scissors and inexperienced children may prove expensive in the long run. A large pair of scissors available for adults but barred for children is useful.

Staplers. These are luxuries but most useful. One of the small lightweight ones is invaluable for joins when glue would not be strong enough and pins would be dangerous. Children have fun just playing with them, making tiny books and envelopes.

Organizing a paper play session. All parents wonder at some time or other how making three feet of paper chain can lead to paper scraps in every room, glue on the stairs, and an amateur haircut. There are one or two helpful tricks. Try to use a chair and table the right height for small children; scrape unwanted scraps of paper straight into a cardboard box placed under the table specially for the purpose; place paste pots in the middle of the table on one tray and allow one old toothbrush per child. Limit the number playing to not more than four at any one time unless you have plenty of spare table space and adult helpers. The right number of special pasting aprons will serve this purpose. Apply a few time-and-motion-study rules, e.g. for paper chains ask each child to cut at least twelve strips before starting to paste and provide a box lid to put them in. The natural difference in pace will ensure that not everyone is pasting at one time. Give beginners a hand if they start to flag on the more tedious repetitive jobs—but only after they have had a good try. Make sure that any job that is started is finished even if you have to do the last bit yourself. Insist that the necessary materials for each job are put away before the next is started. It is inevitable that the working table will look messy—so does a cabinetmaker's bench—but train the children not to spread the bits all over the house or playroom. Keep all the raw materials in one container and have a special box for scissors, clean paste pots and brushes, sticky tape, paper clips, and a stapler. It wastes good playing time to have to look for these before each session.

Anyone with more than one child knows how important it is to sign all creations the minute they are finished but, for children who cannot read, use a specific color for the writing and use the same script they will use at school, i.e. a capital first letter followed by small letters. They soon learn to recognize the shape of their own name.

JUNK CREATIONS

Making shaped or three-dimensional objects with a piece of paper can be difficult. If you find some waste material which is already halfway to the shape you need, so much the better. Every home or playgroup should have a box, string bag, or other receptacle in which to keep strong cartons, egg boxes, round cheese boxes, spools, bottle caps of any kind, toothpaste tube caps, paper clips and fasteners, rubber bands, matchboxes, cigarette packets, Christmas cards, plastic flowers thrust upon you with your soap powder, bits of film, cellophane, bits of wood, pieces of old clocks, shoeboxes, bits of lace, bits of material, fringe, cord, ribbon, tubes from paper rolls—anything. If you have childless or improvident neighbors collect their salvage too.

A list of things to make would need a book on that subject alone but as a jumping-off point use bottle caps with a hole in the middle for wheels. Attach them to cartons with large brass paper fasteners (see Fig. 21). Use cheese boxes for larger wheels. Use egg boxes for goggles (fasten them on with elastic stapled to the edges), earphones, men from Mars; or the separate compartments can be used as flower pots for plastic flowers. Use the two halves of a cheese box to make round picture frames and cut the picture from a Christmas card. A cardboard clock is another possibility. Use small cereal cartons for cameras (make a lever and attach with a brass paper fastener). Two toilet roll tubes stuck together make binoculars; pieces from old clocks or clockwork motors add interest to anything. Before you start children off on any project of this kind make sure you have enough raw material to provide whatever each child needs—

Junk play

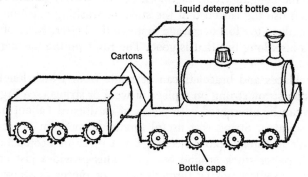

Liquid detergent bottle cap

Cartons

Bottle caps

Papier-mâché beads

Long strip of paper shaped at sides

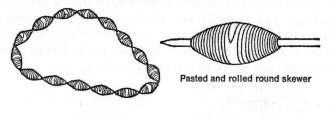

Pasted and rolled round skewer

Picture cut from magazine or
Christmas card pasted to cheese box

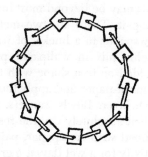

Necklace made from straws and
squares of cardboard threaded on
string or wool

Fig. 21

hence the begging from neighbors. Be bold with regard to size. If you can use the carton that the stove or washing machine came in to make a toy fort or garage so much the better. None of these things lasts long but that is good. The fun is in the making after all.

Necklaces and bracelets can be made from 1-inch lengths of drinking straw strung on a piece of wool or string (see Fig. 21). They can be alternated with pieces of cardboard (about half an inch square). String is a useful threading medium but can be difficult to thread into a needle. Try a piece of Scotch tape or brown paper stuck around one end. This provides just enough stiffness to allow poking through beads or pieces of straw without a needle.

Other raw materials which may be more difficult to find are corrugated cardboard and Styrofoam. Their own peculiar properties make them suitable for all kinds of purposes. If a proper display board for children's work is impossible a large sheet of corrugated cardboard is easy to pin to a door and pictures may be pinned to it. Styrofoam can be carved or cut and used with other things or alone. I have seen it used as framing for children's pictures which looked rather pleasant.

PAPIER-MÂCHÉ

This may be beyond most four-year-olds but older children enjoy using it. There are two methods. One can soak bits of torn-up newspaper in a bucket of water, squeeze it fairly dry, and thoroughly mix in wallpaper paste powder. This should then be molded on to a shape with the fingers. The other way is to tear strips of paper and apply them to the mold, pasting well between each layer. Bowls, saucers, plates, etc. may be used as molds. When absolutely dry the results of either method can be lightly rubbed with sandpaper, painted, and varnished. This is a good activity for a wet day at a grandmother's or on a holiday, as flour paste will do at a pinch, thus the raw materials are easy to provide. Beads made from strips of paper rolled and pasted round a skewer or knitting needle, allowed to dry, and painted are possible for even three-year-olds to manage (see Fig. 21).

COOKING

Children love to help with cooking and can manage some of the simple things alone. Candy made from a stiff mixture of confectioner's sugar and white of egg; cakes made from melted chocolate and cornflakes; candy made from condensed sweetened milk, milk powder, and cocoa powder are all easy. Most five- and six-year-olds will consider it a great treat to be given a commercial cake mix and allowed to get on with it. If they can't read, a bit of help may be necessary but they fairly burst with pride as they hand round these highly-flavored, cardboard-looking objects whose only virtue is that a child can manage them. Small children could have a bit of pastry to shape into a turnover to be cooked with the other baking. Most children can shape quite a creditable loaf from dough when given the chance.

Clay and flour and salt dough were included in natural materials. Small children are content to squash up what they make, but as they get older it is possible to use an oven to dry out these materials to give a more permanent finish. One can make a kiln in the garden from leaves and sticks properly arranged but this needs very careful supervision.

Since creation is an integral part of any play activity it is difficult to decide what to include, or more to the point, exclude. Woodwork, playing with blocks, constructional toys—all require imagination and manipulation which are the essence of creation, but I have tried to describe here how to provide basic essentials for making things, turning raw materials into a finished object. The main points are to let children use anything for any purpose within reason (they will learn material limitations from this far more quickly than from being told), not to underestimate their ability, and not to spoil their pleasure by applying adult standards to their results.

8

Developing Manipulative Skill and Coordination

ALL PLAY LEADS TO increasing skill and general coordination just as all play demands an element of imagination and creative ability. There are some toys and play material whose main value lies in providing opportunities for the repetitive procedures small children enjoy so much. They consist of units which can be used in various ways to encourage full muscular development, recognition of shape, size, color, and similarity, and the gaining of adult skills while giving rise to a quiet, absorbing, relaxing game.

CONSTRUCTIONAL MATERIAL

Whichever age group you are providing for, the most important points to look for are a suitable module (or basic size and shape) to ensure versatility and a suitable size of unit for the size of child. A small baby, for instance, needs something large enough to allow for his limited fingering ability and yet small enough for one hand to grasp; the normal cube-shaped block is just about as much as he can manage but is not versatile enough to satisfy him as his skill and imagination develop.

Building blocks. The use and value of large, hollow blocks and the various shaped wooden blocks one can buy was mentioned in Chapter 3. By the age of three most children are ready for a varied set of blocks and will play with them either alone or with other material until well over ten years of age, so it is worth buying good ones. Colors in building blocks are not really a help. Colors can be learned elsewhere and a plain, polished finish is pleasant to look at and touch. The size to buy may be limited by the storage space available as well as the price. It is worth paying a bit extra to have a special container. Some very good sets come in their own duffel bag or wooden truck. If you can't afford this, try a strong apple box or a nylon string bag. If a box container is fitted with wheels it is obviously easier to transport the blocks and it could be played with alone, thus serving two purposes.

For a number of children where money and space allow it is best to provide both solid and hollow blocks. In an ordinary home with ordinary resources and limitations a good choice is solid hardwood blocks of varying shapes and sizes based on a module of 2¼ x 4½ x 1¾ ins. They are adequate in size, come in wholes, halves, triangles, pillars, arches, etc., are virtually indestructible, and make extremely interesting buildings. Most of the good toy manufacturers supply them so it is up to the buyer to choose the most advantageous price. To provide enough for two children to play with at one time will cost between five and eight dollars. If you can afford a second set, large interlocking wooden blocks are good.

To the wooden block possibilities must be added the plastic blocks which are available. Those which are large and interlock by means of circular projections on their top are very good for babies but there is no point in buying them once a child is past three. Lego, the small version of these, is so much more than just building blocks that it should be included with constructional toys rather than plain blocks.

You may decide to make blocks. Making hollow blocks (see Chapter 3) is easy but solid ones are difficult unless the proper machinery is available. It is imperative that the sizes and shapes match exactly, especially for interlocking blocks. Even some of the bought ones do not fit exactly and should be returned to the manufacturer, as nothing is more infuriating to a learner than finding that the material provided is not fit for the purpose.

Improvising blocks is easy if you bear in mind the importance of a module. Detergent cartons or any others which are strong can be stuffed with newspaper to weight them, glued down, and covered with thick brown paper. It should be a simple matter to provide sizes which are half as big again or half as small as the basic size. These don't last forever, naturally, but do fill gaps in playgroup equipment. Shopwindow display material may be useful if your local shop manager will hand it on when he has finished with it. Empty beer cans make a useful, if noisy, building set. Ordinary pieces of wood, well sanded, may be used in addition but, unless the sizes and shapes match, these will not be a suitable substitute for a proper block set.

Construction sets. There are many sets on the market which consist of units which can be joined together to make finished objects. They vary from those which are used to make buildings, e.g. Lego and Minibrix; those which can be used to make simple working models, e.g. Meccano or large wooden versions of it; and such sets as Tinkertoy and other commercial building sets which are used to make abstract versions of anything. These all serve the purpose of developing skill; some give more scope for imagination than others, some are more difficult than others. When providing these for one child you will have to decide how much skill he already has, whether he is ready to make finished looking objects or prefers to make up his own ideas as he goes along, and whether he will prefer buildings to working models. The ages marked on most of these sets are no help at all. At two some children can take a carriage, stroller, or tricycle to pieces both quickly and quietly. At six another child may be only just getting interested in a large wooden constructional set which is jointed together with huge nuts and bolts. You know your own child best and will find a wide range available in size, material, cost, and demanded ability so there should be something to suit everyone. Once you have decided on the type of constructional toy, you can look for one whose parts fit properly together and stay together, and which is strong, well made, has no sharp edges, incorporates tools which will do the job they are required to do, and contains enough material to make a reasonable-size version of whatever it is.

Having bought your set and got it home, you will probably

find that the box it came in soon collapses. Metal candy and cracker boxes are well worth keeping for this purpose and if you can collect boxes of the same size they will stack more easily in a cupboard or on a shelf. Even if you have to buy a tin box and paint it you will probably save more than its cost in tidiness and convenience.

If you have to provide for a number of children, it is best to have various construction sets to cover a range of abilities and interests. Making them is not particularly easy, but if you keep all the bits and pieces listed under junk play the children will construct quite happily with these. Matchboxes make a perfectly adequate construction set.

Constructional toys. This term is used to cover those toys such as fire engines, tractors, buses, trucks, and trains which come to pieces and can be reassembled time and again. They vary in complexity but children learn to put them together surprisingly quickly and enjoy the repetition. They are available in wood or plastic and in a wide price range. Obviously one should choose one which is well made, strong, has no weak parts and is just within the child's present capability. They are certainly not essential, but if you do have the money or have them given all children appreciate them.

One-action toys. Screw toys, hammer peg toys, interlocking plastic shapes, nesting cubes or shapes, and beads for threading are very good for young children. Some children will still like them at three, four, and five but it seems a pity to buy them once a child has reached three. If you have a child who enjoys this type of activity very much give him ordinary clothespins which he can clip around a cake pan. They can be kept in the pan. To paint them, clip them in a row on a piece of cardboard and paint them all at once.

MATCHING GAMES

There are toys to teach shape, color, and number either separately or all together. Some consist of no more than putting a shape in the same shaped hole, some combine color, shape, and fittings in the same toy. These things can be done time and time again for their own sake or played as a game as with picture dominoes. "Snap" is one of the oldest card games and still a favorite. "Old Maid" is another game which encourages recognition of sets and teaches the protocol of a shared game at the same time. There are games which require previous experience before the child can play, e.g. matching up pictures of furniture for a specific room background, or those which teach by trial and error, e.g. fitting shapes drilled with a number of holes over the appropriate number of doweling pegs. There are sets of pictures to place in a sequence to tell a story, thus requiring and exercising logical ability, and there are picture puzzles which are self-correcting as there is only one place in which each piece will fit.

Which to buy. If you apply one or two criteria to this seemingly bewildering array of games you can soon decide which to choose. Games intended for shape-matching should include plenty of shapes which are easily distinguishable from each other. Those which teach color-matching should have many colors to offer—not just the primary ones. Those which teach grading sizes should have a wide range of size and the shape of their pieces should be commensurate with their place in the scale. (There are one or two sets I have come across which are in scaled sizes but interlock by having large projections to enable them to fit into each other. Thus a piece when separate can look very different from when it is integrated into the interlocked group.) Picture cards or games should have good clear pictures and colors and a uniform style, e.g. a lifelike battleship picture mixed with a set of wooden toy pictures is obviously incongruous and due to bad designing, but this sort of thing does happen. Basic materials and construction should be adequate for the amount of handling they will get and the box or container should be replaced with a suitable one before it falls to pieces.

How to make matching games. Color- and shape-matching sets are very easy to make. Plywood and hardboard if there is a jigsaw available or strong cardboard if not are quite adequate.

For shape-matching, the double-layered tray with shapes cut from the top layer is quick and economical (see Fig. 22). When planning the shapes use a circle for the basic size so that they match in area. This two-layer technique can be used for grading sizes too. Only one lot of cutting is required for both hole and shape, and impact adhesive is all that is necessary to join the two layers.

Color-matching sets can be tiles of strong cardboard, or spool units work well. Colored sticky paper is an easier and more economical coloring matter than paint, if applied carefully lasts a long time, and can always be replaced when necessary. Tiles may be made any size and shape but 2 inches square is a good basic size. To make a spool unit for color-matching or counting, mount lengths of doweling rod in holes drilled in a base of softwood or plywood. The relevant number of spools should be placed on and the exact desired height marked off. The rods can then be cut with pruning shears and the ends rounded off with sandpaper (see Fig. 22). For just color-matching, two spools should be covered in each color and these can then be stood on the doweling pegs in pairs. For counting, cover one spool with one color, two spools with another, and so on and grade the height of the doweling rods accordingly.

Dominoes, either picture or number, can be made from hardboard, wood, or cardboard. Small children enjoy large ones so be generous with the size: 2 ins. x 4 ins. is a good average. One can paint on them or stick on transfers to make the designs (see Fig. 22). Do decide what you are going to keep them in before you settle on the size. Looking for a special size box afterward can take time.

If you wish to paint a background color on wooden shapes, cut them out first, lay them together, and paint over the whole lot at once. Save all the cardboard from strong boxes or from glossy calendars and borrow a paper-cutter to do the cutting. These games are fun to invent and make and needn't cost anything but a packet of colored sticky paper.

It is possible to encourage the learning of color, shape, and number with guessing games of the same type as "I Spy." Four-year-olds can play "I spy with my little eye something colored

Matching, number recognition, and manipulative play

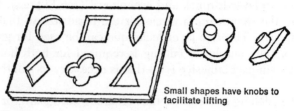

Small shapes have knobs to
facilitate lifting

Shapes
Tray made o. a layer of plywood
from which shapes have been cut.
Stick on to a layer of hardwood.

Number grading
Graded-size doweling pegs
to take large beads, colored
spools, or building cubes
drilled through.
Doweling rods should be just
the right size for the correct
number of beads

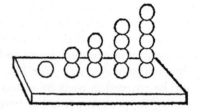

Dominoes

2"x4", made of hardboard or cardboard,
with sticky paper positive and negative
shapes

Lacing cards to make
Simple design with holes punched in
outline. It is important to make a
faint outline on the wrong side, too. Use
plastic-covered wire instead of wool
for beginners.

Fig. 22

red, blue, or yellow, etc." Most of them manage "I'm thinking of something round which grows on a tree" or use numbers as in "I'm thinking of something which has two legs and walks," with a bit of help until they get the idea. These games are useful for car journeys. If it gets too noisy it could be changed for a quieter version such as watching out for three objects of a specific color.

Jigsaw puzzles. These are one of the oldest types of matching game and their value is obvious. They require a child to use his knowledge of color and shape, such logic as he has acquired (even little children can pick out the corner and edge pieces), and his manipulative skill, besides providing an opportunity for the repetition he enjoys so much. Modern jigsaws for children are available in extremely good designs. The simplest ones are pieces to fit into shaped holes in a picture tray. The pieces may even have knobs on to facilitate handling. They progress from one-whole-picture pieces, to simple shapes cut into four or five pieces, to the whole picture and background being removable in pieces from a tray frame. These are usually made of plywood glued on to a hardboard base and most of them have good pictures in good colors.

Once children can manage these, they can go on to the conventional jigsaws made from thick plywood and having an increasing number of pieces. Young children need everything large, clear, and simple. Poky pictures and muddy colors are useless as are those 2,000-piece puzzles made of inadequate cardboard.

It is possible to buy or make hardboard trays on which to make and keep jigsaws. The hardboard is edged with quarter-round molding, allowing a ¼-inch of play for lifting out the first pieces. It helps with clearing up if you put a code color or letter on the back of each piece of a puzzle and the total number of pieces. Thus if you have one piece lettered E 16 in orange you know you must look for fifteen more pieces marked with the same color and symbols.

Jigsaws are easy to make from plywood or cardboard if you only need a few large pieces. It would be tedious to make one of more than twelves pieces. Simple shapes cut from a piece of plywood made into a tray by backing it with hardboard can be drawn or copied from pictures (see Fig. 23). A stout piece of cardboard could have a simple picture pasted to it before cutting it into shapes. Another good idea is using two identical pictures—one stuck on the background tray and one mounted on the material which is to be cut in pieces. Thus children have an additional help, as they can match the bits to the background in addition to each other. Picture postcards can be used for this purpose. A very good puzzle is made by separating a large board into postcard-size units with half-round molding, gluing one of each pair of postcards on the background and mounting the others on the material to make the pieces (this may be hardboard, plywood, or cardboard). The first picture is cut into two pieces, the second into three pieces, the third into four

Picture puzzles

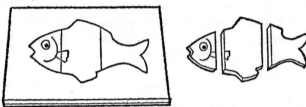

Simple shape cut from a layer of plywood.
The negative shape is backed with hardboard.
The positive shape is cut into three or
four large pieces

— Molding

Graded jigsaw puzzle made on one large tray, using
picture postcards as the picture material

Fig. 23

pieces and so on, so that you have a graded set of puzzles that allows a child to achieve at least one finished picture, however inexperienced he is (see Fig. 23).

One type of picture puzzle is available on cube blocks. Once one complete picture has been assembled by laying the right blocks side by side, the other pictures can be revealed by turning each row in the same direction.

Sorting games. There is a tremendous variety of material produced specially or which can be used for sorting games: colored marbles, sets of tiny objects such as cars, aeroplanes, trees, animals. Beads for stringing can be used for sorting into colors and shapes while making necklaces and bracelets. Most of the shape- and color-matching material can be used in this way. The simplest and cheapest version is to give the children the button box and let them sort out colors and sizes into a sectioned egg carton. Tidying the cutlery drawer, if they can be trusted with the knives, is useful as well as instructive.

PREFABRICATED PICTURE MATERIAL

Bought games such as Fuzzy Felts and drawing templates should not be allowed to take the place of creating pictures from raw materials, but they have some value as a manipulative play material. Children can make a large picture to illustrate a story or nursery rhyme very quickly or they can interpret a particular concept such as number or shape by using ready-prepared units when they might not have enough knowledge or skill to do this alone.

Fuzzy Felts. These sets use the "sticking" power of felt to enable children to fix felt shapes temporarily to a rough or fuzzy background. These sets are reasonably cheap to buy but the units and background base tend to be much too small and fiddly for small children to manage. They are easy and cheap to make. A rough background can be made from felt, flannel, or a thin layer of plastic foam stuck to hardboard or cardboard. Units may be cut from the same fabrics in various colors. When cutting animal or building shapes to be used together, some effort should be made to correlate the various sizes. Pictures cut from cards or paper shapes cut from a catalog and stuck on to cardboard may be used if a tiny piece of emery paper is stuck to the back. The children could help to cut out all the teapots or kettles from a catalog to make a sorting game. Pictures of clothing or furniture to collect into sets is another favorite. If space is difficult it should be possible to fix a sheet of felt to an easel or blackboard to use when the children need a change.

Templates (shapes to draw around). These may be bought made of cardboard, plywood, or transparent plastic. If a number of children are making Christmas cards, then a homemade cardboard template certainly speeds up the proceedings. Another way of reproducing shapes is using tracing paper. The picture to be traced and the tracing paper must be firmly clamped together. The easiest way to do this is by using paper clips at all the corners and the sides too if the picture is large. The main value of these picture-making aids is in encouraging control of a pencil and making a quick, accurate result possible. Some children enjoy them but it is a mistake to have them available every time they want to draw.

Mosaics. These are shaped tiles in varied colors which may be fitted together to make patterns. Most of the toy sets have only geometrical shapes. Some are made of wood. The ¼-inch thick ones are best as the ⅛-inch ones snap easily. If holes are drilled in them they can be fixed in patterns on a piece of fiberboard with short nails. The thickest cardboard versions are obviously better than thin ones and hardboard is better still. Bought ones of a reasonable size for small children are expensive. A quarter's worth of hardboard would provide a very adequate set of large tiles (about 3 ins. across for the square ones and all the others made to match). When all the shapes have been cut, an undercoat of primer paint brushed on all of them at once will leave a suitable surface on which to apply odd bits of paint left over from decorating. Don't use too many colors or there may not be enough similar tiles to make up a pattern.

Preplanned shapes. One can buy cards punched with holes so that laces or wool threaded through them will make a simple outline shape (see Fig. 22). These provide finger exercise which has a concrete result, and are a useful addition to the toy cupboard but are by no means essential. The cards do not last long and it would be cheaper to make them. If they have to last a number of children for a number of years, hardboard might be a good investment.

Similar game is joining up a dotted outline with pencil marks. Older children use numbered dots. One can buy books of these or make them. Most children's comics have a puzzle page which includes this type of thing. If these pages can be collected and stuck on to cardboard they make a useful addition to playgroup material although they do not last long. Other puzzles which help children to handle a pencil while using their eyes and logical ability are mazes. Pictures to finish are very good practice and the children love doing them. One can progress from a teapot which needs a spout to a bird's nest which needs four eggs in it and so on until the children are ready to do such complicated things as drawing all the clothes on to the outline of a body or picking out an odd object from a number of complete ones. This can be done on a blackboard or on a piece of paper, whichever is most convenient, or there are books to buy which have these pictures all ready prepared.

NUMBER RECOGNITION

There is no point in pushing a child to learn to read and write or do formal sums until he is ready but there is no point in holding him back once he wants to learn. Children develop a sense of number far earlier than they learn to recognize the written symbols we use. This means that parents do a great deal of the early teaching of numbers whether deliberately or inadvertently. Special apparatus is available but up to the age of five is not necessary. Peg boards are good but holes should be far enough apart to allow for chubby fingers. Shells, buttons, matchsticks, spools all suffice for counting material. When the children are socially ready to play games, Picture Lotto and Dominoes play a very useful role. Fuzzy Felt units are quick and easy to use. It is important that number is accepted as just a qualifying class and not related to one type of unit only. For this reason, many different counting materials varying in shape and size should be provided.

Children can see without the need for words what size means if they are allowed to lay out ten cereal cartons by the side of ten matchboxes. Arithmetical or geometrical progressions are beyond most preschool children if explained in words but the pattern made by colored units when laid out in ascending or descending numbers is appreciated by a four-year-old. This sense or instinct for number will stand children in good stead when they start doing formal arithmetic at school.

Most of the special material used in preschool or nursery schools such as rods, cubes, and sticks is too expensive and not necessary for home use. Once children recognize the shape of numbers there are many games to be improvised. A good one is a fishing box. The box, decorated with a sea picture, contains cardboard fish each having a paper clip nose. A magnet fishing rod is used to pull out one fish at a time and the children do whatever the instruction written on the fish indicates. For number games this would be a simple sum. The principle can be adopted for reading and writing games later on. Another number game is drawing five apples on the outline of a tree, or ten goldfish in a bowl, and so on.

EQUIPMENT FOR TEACHING ADULT SKILLS

There are one or two difficult activities where simple apparatus or procedures can be a help.

Dressing aids. Defining the front of knit shirts, pullovers, and elastic-topped trousers can be done by marking them with colored thread or wool. Boots and shoes can be treated similarly by marking all the left ones with a color. Gloves can be fastened to a long tape which threads through coat sleeves and across the shoulders so that they don't get lost. Lay out clothes so that they are in the right order for putting on next morning. A long shoehorn is a boon for close-fitting shoes.

Fastenings. Some children have great difficulty in managing buckles on belts and shoes. Make sure the buckle is not too stiff and provide easily accessible practice in the form of a buckled satchel. Most children have difficulty tying bows, especially with shoelaces. They are obviously going to have plenty of practice doing up their laces eventually, but sometimes children are rather solid around the middle and find it impossible to bend enough to get close to the shoe when it is on the foot. It might help in these cases to provide a hardboard shape of a shoe with holes drilled in to take a threaded shoelace. They can then practice on a table which at least helps them to make the necessary complicated movements at a comfortable height.

Where possible use zippers and heavy-gauge grippers instead of buttons. Where buttons are necessary they should be large and the buttonhole should be on the big side. It is important that children are given time to practice these things. Getting ready for a shopping expedition or walk should be started in good time so the children can dress themselves. Time and patience on the part of the mother when the child wants to be independent is very necessary. If that vital stage is missed by being perpetually in a rush, children will eventually prefer to wait to be buttoned up by someone else. If you find it difficult to find the right words to explain the procedures to a child, get another child to show him what to do. They are remarkably good at communicating by showing.

Telling the time. Most children are interested in clocks long before they know which numbers are which. They can remember simple combinations of numbers and hand positions if they are related to mealtimes, bedtime, and so on. Clock faces can be bought or made from cardboard. For small children the simpler they are the better, although it is misleading to simplify to the extent of using only the hour hand. Once they know the numbers and which is the hour hand, you can mark off the quarter hours and teach them "nearly quarter past" or "just after half past" which gives quite an adequate range of times. If you have an old clock children will love to play with it and will see for themselves the relationship of the hour and minute hands.

Between the ages of three and seven children make great advances in acquiring coordination of brain, eye, and muscle. They need time, material, and tactful help during this period. Until they have acquired basic skills they cannot be independent or truly creative and whatever other attributes they possess cannot be used to the full extent.

9

Music

THERE ARE three aspects to music for the preschool child. Music to listen to, music to make, and music to use. Small children apply very different standards to music they will listen to and the music they make. The only common factor is a pronounced and simple rhythm. Once children reach the age of seven they are ready for the limited formality of a percussion band as a group activity and piano lessons individually. Before that age musical experience depends very largely on what is provided by adults.

MUSIC TO LISTEN TO

Parents with musical ability and interests usually provide their children with full opportunity to listen to and learn to appreciate music. Those who can make music are especially fortunate as they can fulfill needs as they arise and can simplify or elaborate as necessary to suit the children's age and listening power. Three-year-olds learning the tune of a nursery rhyme need to hear the melody only until they have the tune firmly fixed. Once they can sing the tune they enjoy a proper piano accompaniment.

Those of us who are not so talented have to rely on record players and records if we wish to control the music we hear. These costly pieces of equipment must certainly not be left for children to use by themselves but it is worth buying some records not necessarily to one's own taste if they will help children develop the listening habit at an early age. Most composers produce some sugarplum pieces which will delight children and not offend the "middle brow." *The Nutcracker Suite, Peter and the Wolf,* lively overtures (especially played by a good, loud brass band) are just a few examples of what small children usually like. Recurring themes, rich melodies, strong rhythms, and full-bodied sound are the qualities to look for.

Music produced specially for children is not always successful. Nursery rhymes lost in the pomposity of harmony, rounds, and opera-like presentation are dreary to someone just interested in the simple tale and tune with which they are familiar. A lively rhythm, traditional tunes, and a wide selection of songs is all they need.

Most jazz music is beyond small children but some seven-year-olds enjoy the rhythms and more exciting melodies of traditional jazz. There are three-year-olds who can twist with the best of us, so there is no need to exclude "pop" music from their program. Since we hear so much of this from other sources it is hardly necessary to buy it for planned sessions, however. It will soon be obvious to an observer which music particular children like or are not interested in and one should provide accordingly, but don't exclude anything until they have tried and not appreciated it. One can include more complicated music as their taste and listening capacity grows.

Musical purists tend to disapprove but children love to have one of the old wind-up phonographs for their own with a supply of discarded 78 r.p.m. records. Viewed solely as cheerful noise makers they have no equal. They cost very little to buy second-hand and the children soon learn the mechanical procedures necessary to operate them alone. Military marches, lively dance music, and folk songs are top favorites in my experience. Most grannies or greataunts will provide a selection of these and the old semireligious songs which were so popular for the Sunday-night-in-the-parlor music sessions in their day. When the spring finally gives out and can't be mended any more, these old phonographs are a rich source of junk play so one really does get the money's worth from them.

MUSIC TO MAKE

Very young children cannot manage a rhythm unless they can do
it at their own pace. This means that cooperating to the extent
required by a percussion band is beyond them. They enjoy just
making a noise or accompanying piano or phonograph music,
although the standard reached seems very low to an adult. As
adults we should remember that the noises we can make would
probably seem of a very low standard to a concert performer and
we should therefore not judge too harshly. If it is a question of
not being able to stand the noise, that is a different matter and
should be treated in a constructive way (e.g. laying down rules
about where and when such noise should be made).

Musical instruments may be bought, the quality varying
greatly with price. One should not expect a toy to make the same
quality sound as a proper instrument. One school of thought
insists on proper instruments or nothing. Other people feel that
children are mainly interested in the noise and, so long as one
does not imply that toy substitutes produce sound to be accepted
as true music, there is no harm in providing bought, made, or
improvised noise makers. The range of sound possible from these
improvised instruments is wide and interesting in its own right.

These playthings may be provided for one child on the spur of
the moment and discarded as soon as interest is lost or may be
permanent fixtures in the toy box for use alone or with other
games. Where a number of children play together, either as a
large family or as a playgroup, a selection of instruments can be
offered for impromptu play, as adjuncts to other play (e.g. a
soldier's drum), or as a separate activity (e.g. when singing
nursery rhymes or round games.)

Drums. Metal drums, either homemade or bought, make a very
loud noise which is not at all drumlike. A layer of cork stuck over
the metal dampens the noise and makes it more realistic.
Stretched rubber is still not drumlike but is easier on the ears.

Drums can be made from round tin containers with the lids
taped on and a cord threaded through to provide a halter.

Remember to stick on the cork layer before letting the children loose with them. Sticks can be doweling rods, bamboo pieces, or any other strong rod with a chamois leather knob stuffed with rags tied to the ends. Another method of making a hand drum is to use an open-ended cylinder (made from a can which has had its ends removed with one of the safety can openers) and stretching rubber from an inner tube over the ends (see Fig. 24). These do not last long but the rubber can be replaced.

Large drums or tomtoms are great fun if you have room to store them. A small barrel covered with stretched rubber and gaily painted makes a most attractive drum.

The main problem with drums is that everyone wants the drum at once. The secret is to provide other instruments which are even larger and more gaily colored so that they have an equal attraction. It is no good offering a three-inch shaker to a child who covets a two-foot drum.

Shakers. Shakers can be made from a wide variety of empty containers to make a number of sounds (see Fig. 24). Talcum powder tins, plastic bottles either of an Indian club shape or with a doweling handle stuck into the opening, pieces of plastic bottle stuck together to make interesting shapes, empty scouring powder cans or other cans stuck on either end of a doweling rod to make a double shaker—all make varying noises. If the "rattle" material is varied, e.g. gravel, nails, rice, dried peas, marbles, an even wider range of sound is possible. The basic procedure is to clean the container thoroughly, put in the rattling material, fasten the lid on securely or add a doweling rod or handle made from an old toothbrush or knife handle if necessary, and decorate gaily. Ordinary enamel paints are adequate. Colored sticky paper patterns will do if the finished surface is varnished over. Shakers can be made from plastic egg cups stuck together or tea strainers fastened face to face, but they really are not big enough if they have to compete with more attractive instruments.

Banging instruments. Triangles are the most common instrument found in pre- or nursery-school percussion bands. These can be bought for use at home but may just as well be improvised from

Drums

  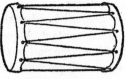

Barrel covered with rubber and decorated

Drumstick. Doweling and knob of chamois leather

Cylinder with both ends covered with rubber and crossed cords threaded through holes

Tumblers filled with water

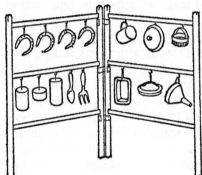

Banging instruments

Collection of sounds for experimenting. Horseshoes mounted on tape

Shakers

Plain-shape plastic bottle with doweling handle

Plastic bottle which is suitable shape without adding a handle

Shaker made from a scouring powder can

Bells

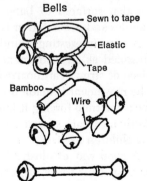

Sewn to tape

Elastic

Tape

Bamboo

Wire

Bells on bamboo or stick

Fig. 24

a horseshoe if you can acquire an old one. After thorough cleaning, all it needs is a loop of tape from one hole large enough to go over a small hand without being so tight that the hand and metal are in contact. A good ringing sound is achieved by banging it with a large nail or some other metal object. A collection of horseshoes will provide different sounds which the children find fascinating.

Cymbals and tambourines are other school favorites and it is difficult to improvise them with any degree of success. The true ringing tone of brass cymbals is an exciting experience for children. Banging two tin plates together is not a good substitute for the noise although children enjoy the movement in the same way. It is possible to make a tambourine-type instrument from paper plates stapled face to face or by using a shallow cylinder from a candy box and covering its ends with parchment or rubber. These are good for one afternoon's making and using but that is their limit as far as being an instrument goes.

If children are simply concerned with banging out a rhythm or if you find you are short of instruments when all the children want to play at once, a tin plate and spoon, two spoons, or two doweling rods to bang together will be useful additions. Fasten a swishy cascade of paper streamers to the end of the sticks with sticky tape to add importance both visually and aurally.

Clappers may be bought but all they are essentially is two wooden surfaces to bang together. Cigar box lids fitted with handles and decorated or two wooden spoons will do.

A very interesting sound effect (which could not possibly be classified as an instrument) is made by holding a fairly strong piece of strong cardboard between both hands and wobbling it. The movement is made by applying pressure to the edges and at the same time forcing it into an arc very quickly. This is easier to do than explain so you must try it for yourself first and then let the children try it.

A good way of illustrating different sounds for children if you have space is to tie objects varying in material, size, shape, and nature to a clotheshorse or suspended batten and provide a stick to beat them with (see Fig. 24). Horseshoes, tin plates, bits of wood, empty tins, and strong bottles—if you can trust the chil-

dren that far—make a good start. After that they will bring
things to tie on and try for themselves. Another set of graded
sounds can be made from tumblers or cans filled with varying
quantities of water. This is a good game for a wet afternoon in a
toyless environment as it requires no special equipment and has
the added attraction of water play at the same time.

Bell instruments. Jingle bells vary in price according to size but
the largest cost about a nickel and most toy shops have them or
can get them. Four or five bells sewn on to 5 inches of tape,
which is then made into a loop with elastic, may be placed round
the fingers and the bells jingled by shaking the hand. Another
version is a half-moon of wire from a wire coathanger threaded
with several bells and having its ends firmly bent round a handle
of 4 inches of bamboo cane thus making a D-shape when com-
pleted (see Fig. 24). Bell sticks are also made from bamboo. A
12-inch length of fairly thick bamboo is threaded with 14 inches
of wire and a bell attached to each end of the wire. The extra
inch at each end is just enough to wind round the bell loop.
These bamboo sticks and handles may be brightened up with
stripes of colored sticky tape.

Xylophones, glockenspiels, pianos, recorders. It is possible to buy
small versions of these instruments. The money required to buy
one which gives a reasonable sound is too much to justify class-
ing them as toys or playthings. The toy versions are not by any
means cheap and have a very limited appeal unless some particular child has set his mind on one. On the whole it is better to wait
until children can learn to use a proper instrument.

USING MUSIC

Musical activities are very popular for nursery schools and playgroups and can be enjoyed at home even with only one child.
Nursery rhymes, finger plays, singing games, and movement to
music are all possible at the age of three if kept simple. As
children progress they play or sing the same things but add
variations of their own.

Nursery rhymes. The only basic necessities for singing nursery rhymes are a voice of any kind and a wide repertoire of songs and music. If you can sing well this is an advantage, if you can play the piano this is even better, but these are really not essential gifts. An instrument of some kind is useful for a large number of children when learning new tunes or merely to ensure everybody starting off in more or less the same key. If none of the available adults plays a piano try using a recorder. These are easy to learn and are ideal for simple melodies. Phonograph records may be useful if you choose them carefully. They should not be too elaborate.

There is a very wide selection of books of nursery rhymes. It is worth buying a book with a comprehensive selection even if children prefer their own little books at an early age. Ones which suit the needs and pocket of most parents and groups are *Songs to Grow On* and *Songs for the Nursery School*. They have attractive pictures, and contain some suggestions for finger plays too.

Nursery rhymes may be acted as well as sung and dressing up adds to the fun. This need be no more than a hat or a mask to represent each character, otherwise it takes too long for everybody to have a turn.

Folk songs which are not really rhymes are also popular with small children. They like the lively tunes and the repetition of choruses or the logical, inevitable progression of events. Some of the Gilbert and Sullivan songs are appreciated because they can join in the choruses. Counting songs are useful for children just learning numbers, e.g. "One Little, Two Little, Three Little Indians." The smallest children can be given a job to do until they can join in the counting.

Finger plays. These movement songs demand imagination and improve coordination and this makes them very good for the youngest children. There are special books of them to buy, or some nursery rhyme books give suggestions, but it is very easy to make them up. The movements should not be confined to fingers only but should be as wide and sweeping as space and conditions allow. Fingers depicting the "lovely sunshine which dried up all the rain" for Incey Wincey Spider should start as high and wide as they can be stretched, and the rain should start high and end at one's feet unless this leads to overbalancing or knocking over one's neighbor, at which point the game deteriorates somewhat.

Start the babies off on the ones they probably know already such as "This little pig went to market"; go on to "Two little dicky birds" with fingers representing Peter and Paul. Before long the children should manage quite complicated movements such as "Here is the church, Here is the steeple."

Singing games. Preschool children find complicated folk dance routines beyond them but starting with "Ring around the rosy" they enjoy some games which follow a set pattern. Many from your own schooldays will occur to you and "The farmer's in the dell" or "I wrote a letter to my love" are still top favorites. There is a book called *The Lore and Language of Schoolchildren* * which traces the incidence of certain of these games through generation after generation of schoolchildren. It is a valuable source of play material besides making fascinating reading.

For teaching the tunes a piano or recorder can again be a valuable aid. The children learn the words and tune surprisingly quickly, however, and teach each other. Simple props add to these games: a farmer's hat, a wife's hat, a nurse's hat. They also avoid tension about exactly who was asked to be one of the characters.

Movement to music. There are some movement activities, not nearly as formal as dancing, which are controlled by the type of music provided. The children stamp, skip, or tiptoe as directed by the adult group leader and suggested by the accompanying music. Radio programs provide this kind of service for home or playgroup but with a bit of training or background reading most playgroup supervisors could lead a group in this activity. The children are asked to behave like buses, aeroplanes, elephants, to pretend to sleep, to roll over like a log, and so on. This gives opportunity for muscle exercise and control and for imaginative movement at the same time.

* By I. and P. Opie, Oxford University Press, 1959.

A piano is the ideal instrument but failing this a recorder or even a tambourine can be used to suggest the type of movement. Suitable music from a selection of records will also serve the purpose. If tape recorder apparatus is available, programs or selected music can be recorded to provide a session at any time.

Music is valuable for young children either alone or as an addition to singing and games. If we provide them with a rich musical background, they develop an appreciation for the pattern and variation produced by rhythm, melody, and instruments which is the very essence of music. Whether they turn out to prefer classical or jazz music is really immaterial and certainly beyond our powers to control.

10

Books

STRICTLY SPEAKING books are not play material as, apart from the pop-up or pull-out varieties, they can only be looked at. Their value for quiet periods and the amount of information they impart, albeit at secondhand, is so important that they should have a place in every home or playgroup.

WHAT TO READ

Children at an early age can learn from books about people, countries, and objects they would not otherwise encounter and a great deal of social behavior pattern is imbibed subconsciously from them. For this reason it is important that the content of books is carefully examined before buying. Books which are given can be a problem. One which is really unsuitable should be withheld or exchanged.

Fairy stories and fantasies can obviously have full rein but books offering facts to small children should be checked for authenticity. If the content has had to be simplified to the point of inaccuracy to suit the age group then it is better to wait and present such material when it can be absorbed in a truer version. Pictures should be good and their design should be consistent. Again fairy stories may have fantastic illustrations but if the text says very firmly "A is for apple" the A should not be entwined with flowers and curlicues and the apple should look like an apple. The same criterion should be applied to rather more involved issues. Most people have views on horror pictures but rarely agree on what constitutes horrific. In my experience some picture which appears quite innocuous to an adult can send a child into a frenzy of terror. Others which are quite vicious in content will have absolutely no effect at all. All one can do is buy books which seem acceptable and be prepared to exchange, swap, or give them away if your children can't bear them. Good colors are important in children's books and pictures. All this experience of color, outline, and design is stored away in the subconscious even if it is not put into words. A wide variety of good color and design will provide a basic knowledge for when the children come to design for themselves.

When considering books for the three- to seven-year-old children, age is not an efficient guide. Few children at seven can read fluently enough to manage the long or complicated stories they enjoy and understand when these are read to them. Three-year-olds like to look at books alone as well as listen to short stories. The variety of books available is wide in price, style, and content. Some publishers specialize in children's books which are good and cheap; others produce only expensive classics. Some publish a never-ending flow of cheap trash which is badly written, badly illustrated, and badly produced. The wise adult who has money to spend on books will go to a bookshop, not a toy shop, to investigate before buying. The local public library officials will always give advice on old or new books for different age ranges. Every child should have access to a collection of books comprising old favorites, books within his present capacity, and one or two which are just far enough ahead of him to present a challenge. With the help of the public library, books given for birthdays and Christmas, and such purchases as are within one's means, it should be possible to provide an adequate library without straining financial resources too much.

For those people who do not have a good bookshop near or find catalogs and lists inadequate, I have set out below the basic types of books suitable for preschool children. Appendix A lists titles of books for children from three to five and five to six.

Picture books mainly for looking at. These should have very little text. What there is should be clear, in plain type, and it is best if the pictures and the text are on facing pages.

Books for looking at and reading from. Such books have to be read through at least once so that the child can associate the pictures with the story when he is looking at the book alone.

Books mainly for reading from. These books must still have good illustrations as children always ask to see what characters and objects look like. The main interest is in the text, however.

Books for children just learning to read. These should have a limited vocabulary and a small quantity of text well spaced so that the children soon come to the end of a page and gain some sense of achievement. Plenty of good clear pictures are necessary to provide some help in suggesting what unfamiliar words might be. Type should be plain and clear, using capital and small letters as taught in schools.

Many of the books for "looking at" are in this range too. Some of the readers used in schools are available for parents to buy. There seems little point in encroaching on these, however, as they have little story or information value apart from teaching a basic vocabulary. Most publishers of children's books have a range catering to the learner. Prices and production vary so much that one must choose the best at the price one can afford, bearing in mind all the basic necessities and standards.

Books of nursery rhymes. Small children will enjoy a profusely illustrated book with a limited number of rhymes. Many publishers produce these. As children get older they need a more comprehensive selection to be read from. There is a wide range at around two dollars from which to choose.

Fairy tales. Small children do not like the original Grimm and Andersen stories but enjoy a slightly romanticized version of these classics. Other nationalities have their traditional stories which all hold a certain charm for the five-year-olds and over.

Reference books. All children are interested in the world about them and reference books are a great aid to classification of experience. Even if the text is too advanced for them, just having a source of identification available can lead to continued and extended interest if help is given by adults.

There are many books of reference on any subject one cares to name but they cost a great deal of money and the age range of three to six years would not really benefit enough to justify buying them at this stage, except for the small ones done especially for children. Encyclopedias produced especially for children need a great deal of thought. Some are good and well produced, others are not. Many are expensive. The baby versions produced for small children usually deal inefficiently with too few subjects to justify the name encyclopedia. It is better to have the small, inexpensive books on specific subjects, or to allow access to the adult encyclopedia if you have one. If there is not one in the house it is good training to accustom children to using the reference section of the public library.

Books purely for reading. Some children at nearly seven years old can read or will listen to a full-length book a section at a time. Once they have reached this stage the whole world of literature is open to them. Use of the public library should be encouraged. Where money is limited, a large paperback library is better than one or two beautifully bound classics. If a paperback finally does come to pieces after being read time and again or being lent to friends, it was a good investment and should be replaced. If it remains in pristine condition because it is not appreciated, then a more expensive version would have wasted even more money. The rich essence of a wide experience of literature lies in the mind, not in the bookcase.

WHERE AND WHEN TO READ

The power of concentration is a habit which has to be learned. This must be borne in mind when reading provision is made for children. A quiet, relaxed atmosphere in a place removed from other distracting activities is necessary for small children. Eventually one hopes they will develop the gift of being lost to all else which is so valuable to the reader if infuriating to others. Some comfortable corner where there is a place to rest the book either on a table or low stool is suitable. A small-size book can be a help to learners as it is difficult to hold and turn over the pages of the larger ones. At home a well-lit corner of the room could be accepted by the reader and others as a quiet retreat where he will be allowed to finish the story without interruption. Children over five may prefer to retire to their bedroom. The main aid is a tacit acceptance by child and adult that there is a "do not disturb" rule which applies to every member of the household when reading.

A reading corner is a must in a playgroup. This should be in a good light and if possible screened off from other activities. A folding bookcase which may also be used as a screen is a useful piece of equipment. Small chairs and a table or tuffets and an orange box will do as furniture.

When to read depends on whether the children are to look alone or to be read to. Not many mothers can read on demand as they have other responsibilities, but some definite part of the day should be set aside when children can rely on having a story. After lunch or just before bedtime or both is the normal routine as this allows food to be digested at times when energy is at a low ebb for both mother and children. In playgroups, after mid-morning milk is a good time as a group of children will all be wanting to start some new activity at once and can listen to the story from the beginning. As more adults are available than at home, stories need not necessarily be limited, however. Books should be available to children at all times and low bookshelves where they can be properly displayed are better than a box of books. These shelves need not be elaborate.

Bookshelves may be bought as fixtures or as movable units which swing out from the wall to make a reading corner. If space is short one can buy shallow, hinged sets of shelves which fold to about 9 inches wide and when open form a display unit and reading corner at the same time (see Fig. 25).

All these ideas can be copied or improvised. An old-fashioned clotheshorse covered in with hardboard and having curtain wire rails placed just above the battens will serve as screen, book-shelf, and the bookstore (see Fig. 25). When folded this takes

Bookshelves to make or buy

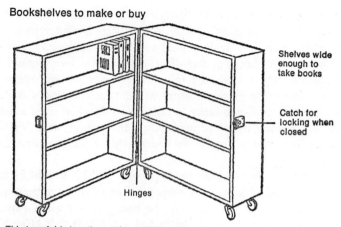

Shelves wide enough to take books

Catch for locking when closed

Hinges

This type folds together at the end of the session, serves as storage, and provides a screen

To make or improvise

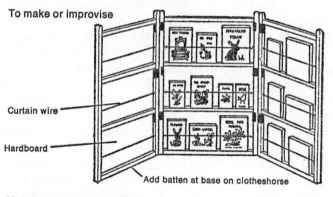

Curtain wire

Hardboard

Add batten at base on clotheshorse

Made from covered clotheshorse, or from batten frame covered with hardboard. Provides storage and screen

Fig. 25

very little room. If the hardboard would be too heavy, it could be covered with canvas or material, but it would not be so solid or soundproof. Wall bookshelves can be made from battens and curtain wire as explained in Chapter 2. Apple boxes or orange boxes placed on their sides could provide shelf space and serve as a screen. They could then provide storage space after each session if they have to be put away. A wall pocket-unit made from material is a way of providing temporary display space for books. A playhouse screen used inside out could provide shallow shelves for books in the same way as the clotheshorse. By placing the playhouse several feet away from a corner the space left could be used for reading. Special clips to support shelves are available for use with a peg-board screen. All these ideas are really only necessary for playgroups, but if there is a special playroom in the house they can be very useful for just one or two children.

HOW TO READ STORIES

Some adults are good at this, others are not, but there are one or two tricks which might be helpful in the latter case. Choose a story you like yourself otherwise you will find that yawns, bleary eyes, and a tendency to produce Spoonerisms will make you uncomfortable and ruin the session for the listener. A good clear voice and diction is essential but do not project the voice too much or talk too loudly, particularly for one child. It is pleasant if you can produce a slightly different voice for each character but don't make this so complicated that you forget which is which. The children will lose no time in pointing this out. Interruptions from small children are inevitable. If they are enjoying the story they butt in automatically as their minds race ahead and this is a good sign. They may wish you to elaborate on a point not specially touched on in the story. It is better to ask them what they think about this and use their version, as someone else may read the same story to them afterward and it is confusing if the grown-ups give different accounts. For this same reason do not be tempted to change words you do not particularly like. Children remember word for word what was read last time and they hate arbitrary changes. If, after some discussion about the story, it is difficult to regain the attention of a group of children, a good trick is to say "look at me." This gives them something positive to do and once there is a focal point to their combined attention you can start again.

Showing pictures as you go along can be difficult. If the book is a good one the text should be related closely in content and position to the pictures. If, for some reason, it is not, finish off a complete section before turning to the relevant picture. Never be bullied or cajoled into letting the book leave your hand. If the group is large and the pictures small, pass the book around at the end of the story. Pictures are useful as a basis for recapitulation and extension and it is always a good plan to allow time for this.

COMICS

Producing comic strips and comic books for children is big business. There are many available for preschool children. None is wholly good but not many are wholly bad. The main advantage to comic strips is that they come through the door regularly without effort on anybody's part and ensure that some new reading matter comes into the house. If you can afford and prefer the "teaching" approach, this is obtainable in comic book form. The best thing to do is to try several before choosing. Make sure you don't detest them as at this age children have to be read to.

Providing our children with suitable reading matter is one way in which we can overcome some of the limitations of our environment. Books provide experience, knowledge, and food for imagination. Dollar for dollar, books are a splendid investment and it is worth taking time and trouble in selecting the best of their kind and showing children how to enjoy them.

11

Storytelling

STORYTELLING is almost certainly the oldest form of entertainment. One person to tell, one person to listen, and nothing else is necessary. In the ancient civilizations storytelling was a means of earning a living. Most storytellers or imparters of information today prefer to communicate by the written word but, for small children, listening is the only method of widening their vocabulary and learning syntax. They can do this by listening to conversation but this is not always suitable or interesting for them. Storytelling can be geared to their age, needs, and interests and, as an activity, is only possible when the teller is giving full attention to the listener thus ensuring the right relationship and atmosphere for learning. Small children also have something to offer the art of storytelling. They have meticulous memories and insist that stories are told word for word and fact for fact at every telling. They are thus guardians of traditional stories and family histories. The variations which occur from generation to generation are due to the time lag between being a listener and a teller and the slips of memory which take place during this period.

Material for stories should never be difficult to find. The most simple little tales or the recounting of some family anecdote will delight small children. They like plenty of repetition within the story, a happy or funny ending, and not too much description. When they reach the stage of wanting to know what color socks Red Riding Hood wore they will suggest this themselves. Ordinary everyday activities can be used as a story framework, e.g. shopping, when the local shops can be used as a background for looking for some specific object which gives plenty of opportunity for "Ting, ting went the shop bell" and "Good morning, Mr. Grocer" and so on, ending up with the triumphant carrying home and eating, using, or playing with whatever the object was. Stories about lost objects give scope for the "But, alas, it was not there" type of chorus. Adults who find even such simple plots difficult to fabricate should listen to the radio and television programs written specially for small children. Pictures from magazines can be used as a basis for a story, or a particular building which the child knows can have a history invented for it. A small notebook which can be given over to synopses of stories for telling is useful for a mother and very necessary for playgroup leaders.

One very useful aspect of storytelling is that it can be used to introduce children to new situations which they might find frightening without proper preparation. It is much better to tell children about what happens when a small child goes to the doctor, dentist, or hospital in story form than just to give him the information as such. A story about what happens to a child of the same name when his mother goes to the hospital to have a new baby is very reassuring to a child in this situation. His unspoken doubts and apprehensions are alleviated without having to be put into words that may well be beyond him. Because the story has a happy ending it is confidently accepted that his mother too will return and that someone will look after him while she is away. The same technique can be used for going into the hospital. Explain how the child in the story was puzzled by the funny smell and the white clothes and the high bed, and what the reasons are. Thus when the time comes your child is not only forewarned of all these strange things and knows why they are necessary but, as each new thing happens, he also feels reassured that events are following a familiar pattern. Using the mythical child also gives children an opportunity to ask questions without acknowledging the doubts and fears as their own. They too can be attributed to the person in the story.

Some events puzzle children for a long time after they have happened and often a story about them helps to present a whole picture which they appreciate more than isolated reassurances. As, for instance, when a playgroup leader has to leave and is replaced by someone else. The children can be told a story about a group of children, giving all their names in turn, who were looked after by Mrs. Smith. One day Mrs. Smith's husband had to go away to work (giving all the details) so she could not look after all the children (giving each name again) any more. Mrs. Smith had a friend who was called Mrs. Jones who said she would look after the children and read books and tell stories to them instead of Mrs. Smith—and so on. Any questions about where Mrs. Smith has gone and whether she looks after another group of children can be settled at the end of the story and after this the group will accept the new leader and very quickly forget the old one. It is the unfinished story which disturbs children. Once they know the end they are quite content to forget it.

Physical handicaps in other people which children notice and ask about can be told about in story form. This should be done before a handicapped child enters the playgroup, stressing how all the other children in the story were patient with the deaf, spastic, or crippled child.

Storytelling can take place anywhere as it involves no equipment whatever. It can be at the request of the child, for some adult motive such as imparting information, or to fill in time when other activities are not possible. As an art and entertainment it has lost none of its virtues with the passing of time and undoubtedly never will.

12

Pets and Yards

LACK OF YARD SPACE and room for large pets must be included with all the other disadvantages of modern living. All children should know about the world they live in, how things grow, and what animals are really like as opposed to how they appear in storybooks. Photographs and television can help to some extent but nothing can reproduce the feel, smell, or noise of a small animal or the true colors and textures of plants and trees. Where possible this lack of necessary experience should be overcome at weekends and holidays and by making use of parks, farms, and zoos. There are some ways in which we can help children in this respect even within a limited environment.

PETS

The role of a pet in a child's life is not easy to define. It is not until the age of seven-plus that the pressure is really put on parents to buy a dog or cat. At this age some children desperately need something to be their undemanding friend, slave, and playmate and their pet becomes part of their personality. From other children who have an easier relationship with their fellows the demands for pets are not so insistent. The preschool child is not capable of looking after or appreciating the needs of a pet and is more concerned with getting to know fellow human beings. Thus the need at this age is for some animal which is not demanding and is not too fragile to play with, but is interesting to watch and will give small children some experience of the animal world.

Choosing a pet. Dogs and cats need a certain amount of room, time, and exercising, and some mess must be anticipated. Fouled yards can be a great nuisance where there are toddlers and babies, especially when the space available is limited. Some dogs or cats may be expensive to feed and this should be borne in mind if money is short. Once one has considered whether the limitations of home, yard, and family would be fair to a cat or dog and whether the advantages outweigh the disadvantages, timing must be considered. Not every member of a docile breed of dog or cat turns out to be docile or sweet-tempered, and puppies and kittens are always more excitable than adult animals. Training of children and animals takes patience and a harassed mother may find dealing with both at the same time quite exhausting. The best thing to do is to have the dog or cat first and hope that it will not be jealous of children when they start affecting the normal animal routine.

Less trouble are those animals which prefer living in an enclosed space and can be kept in a hutch so that contact between them and the children can be controlled. If there is space in the yard, rabbits are very good. The best way to keep them is in a fenced-in run which includes a hutch (see Fig. 26). Children can see what they are doing without interfering too much and the rabbit, while comfortably free, is safely guarded from cats and dogs. Rabbits are cheap to buy and keep and hutches can be made from scrap wood. Guinea pigs are similar to rabbits but need just a hutch, so they can be kept in a yard or shed. They are more expensive than rabbits to buy but are delightful pets.

Indoor pets may be possible if you have no yard. Golden hamsters are most attractive little things, live happily in a small cage indoors, and do not object to being carefully played with now and then. They cost almost nothing to feed and, unlike the other animals, may be left for one or two days with a suitable supply of food and water without attention. Their only drawbacks are initial expense, short life, and nocturnal habits. They are usually willing to come out during the day for food and attention if you train them to this gradually. Mice may not appeal to mothers and tend to smell, however carefully they are

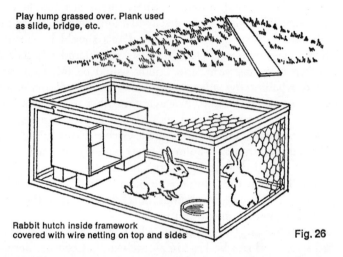

Play hump grassed over. Plank used as slide, bridge, etc.

Rabbit hutch inside framework
covered with wire netting on top and sides

Fig. 26

looked after, but this is less important when they are kept in a
playroom and not a living room. Whatever boys' comics may
suggest, they should not be carried round in pockets.

All pet shops sell small, cheap books on how to look after the
animals they sell and these should be carefully studied before
buying a pet.

If an animal pet is not possible, providing a bird or fish might
be considered. Cage birds are easy to look after and cheap to
feed although expensive to buy and provide with a suitable cage.
Again one should find out how to look after them before buying.
If they are placed where children can see them this is much more
fun than only being able to see the bottom of the cage, although
if there are cats in the household this may not be sensible.
Goldfish, though not terribly interesting as pets, are certainly
better than nothing. One goldfish in a bowl with a piece of water
weed is adequate. A properly fitted aquarium is better. Again,
these should be placed at a suitable height for children, who are
usually very careful about not knocking the bowl or tank even
when placed on a low coffee table.

If pets are absolutely forbidden in playgroup premises it might be possible to import a caged one for one day each week. A bowl of goldfish should not be impossible even here.

Substitutes for pets. When not even a parakeet is possible, the only thing to do is to attract what animals and birds there are to your door or window at some time of the day so your child can see some form of animal life. Scattering breadcrumbs on a garden, yard, or windowsill will suffice in the winter. A bird tray is better though not strictly necessary. Half a coconut or peanuts threaded on a piece of string and hung outside a window should attract small birds for apartment dwellers to watch. A special bird table made on a wooden arm can be attached to a window frame. You must ensure that small children attracted to a window to watch the birds cannot climb or fall out, of course.

Even in an area where pets are banned by landlords, there is always the odd dog or cat somewhere about. Always insist that not all strange animals like being touched and that only well-known ones should be handled. It is a pity to have to do this as it is rare for children to be attacked or bitten and just telling them that it might happen can sap their confidence. It could happen, however, and on balance it is better to warn and explain why, at the same time taking care not to frighten them unduly.

All small children find insects and garden creatures such as worms and snails fascinating. These can be kept in suitable jars with a food and air supply for a time. Frogs' eggs collected from ponds, snails found in a bunch of watercress, slugs found in cabbages, and moth larvae which appear in every garage may not be very prepossessing but at least they illustrate the other possible forms of life. We should not allow our own inhibitions to prevent children learning about these creatures.

GARDENS AND YARDS

The advantages of gardens and yards are obvious. They provide space, fresh air, and opportunity for learning about plants, animals, and trees. Children's needs should be borne in mind especially where space is limited. Flower borders or beds should be left until children are older and even vegetable beds are not so useful as an adequate expanse of grass on which to play.

The ideal is to give children as much room as possible and if they can have a separate play space so much the better. All the adventure equipment should be kept near this area. One very good idea is to make a special hump or hollow by adding or removing earth (see Fig. 26). This gives a defined area and this feature can be incorporated into all kinds of imaginative games. If it is sown with a coarse low-growing grass seed it should stand up to the inevitable wear and tear and not require too much mowing. A piece of stone or an interesting tree trunk is a good addition and need not be unsightly. All the features mentioned in the chapter on Adventure Play should be borne in mind, as should sandpits. Tall growing vegetables such as runner beans can be used to make private and screen off the messy appearance of their area.

Gardens provide growing materials which always interest small children. Once new shoots, leaves, or buds are pointed out to them they learn to look for these changes. Children under seven are usually too impatient to appreciate a garden of their own but they enjoy being allowed to help with adult sowing and reaping activities. Point out the different shapes and colors of leaves so that children learn to distinguish between various plants and trees. Even if they can't remember the names, they enjoy looking up the shapes in a reference book or making a scrapbook from a seed catalog or pressed leaves. This is all good practice in shape matching.

Where gardens are not possible, vacant lots can provide an interest, as can public parks if they are not too formal and forbidding. If only a small yard is available, two or three barrow loads of top soil can be used to make a trough garden or rockery so that some plants can be watched. Window boxes and sink or bowl gardens can be used in apartments. These do not offer a great deal of variation but by providing them in conjunction with mustard and cress grown on flannel, peas and beans grown in a jam jar with wet blotting paper, and bulbs grown in a glass so that the roots show, it should be possible for all children to have some knowledge of how plants grow. These last suggestions should be useful for the most restricted playroom.

Even the vegetable rack holds interest and information. Cabbages cut across the middle never fail to impress small children with their intricacies. Children like taking a lettuce to pieces till they come to the smallest leaves in the middle or looking at an apple cut so that they can see the seeds, peeling bananas or inspecting pea and bean pods. Adults take these things very much for granted but they are full of delight to someone who sees them as objects in their own right, not merely as food to be prepared or cooked; the feel, smell, taste, and appearance are all experience to be recorded and evaluated for future reference. The world around us is an exciting place. It is our job as parents to give our children the opportunity to see this and to teach them to look for and notice nature at work.

13

Children in Bed

REALLY SICK CHILDREN cause anxiety. It is when they are getting better that they cause trouble. Mothers at their lowest ebb from worry, sleepless nights, and running up and down stairs, have to deal with a child not well enough to get up or amuse himself very long, along with other children who are feeling slightly neglected and a house which needs putting in order.

MAKING CHILDREN COMFORTABLE

The most unpleasant aspect of illness for children is being away from the rest of the family and all the things they can hear going on downstairs. If the doctor gives permission it is a great relief to everyone concerned for the child to come downstairs for some part of the day. Housework can then be fitted in so that the child does not feel lonely. If coming downstairs is out of the question, it is a pleasant change to transfer to someone else's bed for some part of the day. This gives a different wall to look at and allows the invalid's room to air. If beds can be placed near a window, or a mirror can be hung at such an angle as to enable the patient to see outside, this is a great help.

A comfortable support can be made with pillows borrowed from all the beds. Make a pile of three pillows one on top of the other in the normal place. Place two more on and at right angles to these and spread them slightly apart at the lower end. Place one more pillow across these two in the same way as the first three. The head and shoulders are supported by this last pillow and the two at right angles support the sides and arms so that the patient is in a close fitting armchair of pillows.

Some kind of tray or bed table is helpful. One can buy proper bed trays or make them but they can be improvised. An ironing board may be the right height. A large but shallow cardboard carton can have pieces cut out of the sides so that it leaves room for the trunk while fitting close up to the chest to act as a table. A small low coffee table might be suitable or a board supported on either side of the bed by means of chair seats made the right height with firm cushions. Provide a box or bag to hold toys so that they are not forever falling on the floor.

POSSIBLE PASTIMES

Those children who can read a little are much easier to entertain than really small ones. Borrowed books will provide a new interest if the disease is not infectious. If it is, buying or begging unfamiliar comics and cheap books which can be burned will do. Activities for little children can be the same as usual with different or new materials if possible.

Making pictures. All the usual picture-making games—using pencils, crayons, felt-tipped pens and colored sticky paper, lacing cards, joining dots, and filling in outlines—can be played with but paint should be avoided. Large pictures are possible and give a continuing interest if they are made bit by bit on the collage principle. Scrapbooks work best if all the pieces are cut out first and the pasting left until help is available. Salt pictures are easy to make and provide a change. A large, deep-sided baking pan lined with dark paper, a plastic glass, a sheet of newspaper, and a large salt cellar full of dry salt are necessary. The newspaper is spread over the counterpane just in case any salt is spilled. The pattern or drawing is made by allowing salt to flow on to the dark paper. To wipe out the picture or re-collect the salt when the cellar is empty, the pan can be emptied from one corner into the plastic glass. By squashing the glass to form a funnel, the salt can be replaced in the salt cellar. Most intricate patterns can be made with virtually no effort or conscious thought. Fuzzy Felts, templates, and stencils help to produce other pictures without needing much effort.

Paper games. Paste is not a good idea when playing in bed unless supervision is available, but folded paper objects are very useful. Paper boats, decorated circles cut and stapled to make wigwams or hats, boxes made from mitered squares, or any of the simple Origami objects will keep children occupied for quite a long time. A stapler is invaluable. Making a picture for each member of the family and an envelope to put it in takes a long time. Cutting paper patterns in bed is possible but a careful eye should be kept on even round-ended scissors as sick children often doze off in the middle of cutting and leave the blades apart. Pretending to wrap up Christmas presents may amuse them if you have any leftover paper and small cartons.

A set of cardboard units cut from a cereal box and a packet of colored sticky paper shapes will provide the raw material for a new set of dominoes or counting cards which the children can make for themselves. A cardboard doll-shape can be clothed with paper shapes cut from patterned papers using a template for the basic dress- or hat-shape. These paper garments fasten on with tabs which fold down at the shoulders and sides. Sets of these can be bought from most toy shops if there is not time or the child is not able to make them.

Junk play. All the items and suggestions under this heading in Chapter 7 can be used by children in bed. Necklaces made from pieces of drinking straw, poppit beads, wooden beads, or proper beads from a broken necklace are very popular. Paper clips can be strung together by the smallest children.

Dolls. Ordinary size dolls and cots are too big to play with in bed but a small set contrived from a chocolate box bed, folded handkerchiefs for pillows and sheets, small pieces of shiny material or wool pinked at the edges for counterpanes, and a pipe-cleaner doll will provide one afternoon's fun. Bigger children could probably make the doll themselves. One looped strip for the head and neck, one bent round the neck to form two arms, one bent double to form the trunk, and one for each leg and looped foot, strengthened and padded with gummed paper strip, make quite a sturdy little doll which can be draped around with a handkerchief or lengths of colored ribbon.

Puppets. New puppets are a great delight and are useful as a stationary activity. They can be made or improvised very quickly (see section on puppets in Chapter 4). Older children can entertain themselves with a puppet show if you place a mirror in such a way that the reflection faces them. A carton theater placed on a makeshift bed table will make a suitable frame for their activities. A similar pastime is making shadow pictures on the wall. Cut-out shapes attached to doweling handles can be made to perform all kinds of actions if a reading lamp is put in the right place. A little experimenting is necessary before making pictures with hands and fingers is possible.

Knitting and sewing. Not many young children can knit properly but spool knitting, using four nails knocked into a spool, is possible even for some four-year-olds. The results can be sewn into a round mat for the dollhouse or a doll's hat. Raffia or thick wool can be used for weaving mats or wrapping round 1-inch cardboard cylinders to make napkin rings. Weaving cards may be made from round or rectangular pieces of cardboard with serrated edges.

Felt pictures can be made from scraps of felt cut into shapes and stuck to a felt or cloth background with a suitable adhesive. This needs help, especially with the sticking. Pot-holder mittens may be made in the same way.

ENTERTAINING THE IMMOBILE CHILD

There may be times when sick children are not able to move or do very much for themselves because of a handicap, acute illness, or even sheer exhaustion. If immobility is due to purely mechanical reasons and the child is otherwise normal, this can be a very trying time for the whole family. Something to watch is the only answer and birds attracted to the windowsill or even a special bird table made for the purpose will help the day along. Goldfish in a bowl or tank provide another interest. Swishy streamers or a balloon or paper windmill fastened outside the window to be caught and moved by the wind is another good idea. If the child is able to hold and switch a flashlight on and off he can have a good deal of fun especially with one which changes color or size of beam. Mobiles to hang from the ceiling may be bought or homemade. A kaleidoscope is useful. Binoculars or a magnifying glass will provide interest from quite ordinary objects without too much activity on the part of the child.

When eyes are damaged or not to be used for some reason the problem becomes even more acute. It is possible to buy sets of wind chimes to hang outside windows but they are rather expensive. Phonographs and radio programs are useful. Guessing games of things to feel are possible if there is someone to play with. Matching-shape games can be played just by touch especially the large-size baby versions. Large wooden beads can be threaded on to plastic-covered wire.

It would be foolish to imply that any of these suggestions can provide more than twenty minutes' diversion at any one time. If it is possible to do just the bare necessities of cooking and looking after other children, it might be better for the weary mother to buy a supply of knitting wool and move an armchair into the child's bedroom. She will rest her body and achieve something that way and the sick child will recover more quickly for the attention he receives. The other children can join in the games and the reproach of a neglected house is at least a silent one.

14

Planning a Successful Playgroup

PLAYGROUPS set up to cater to the play needs of a specific age group must acknowledge that, while their function is limited to providing suitable opportunity for play experience, their responsibility in this one field is greater than that of the mother's. Playgroups must provide the large equipment, varied activities, a wide choice of possible friends, and the space for which modern living conditions leave no room. Special attention must be paid to equipment, use of space and time, creating a happy atmosphere, and the role of adults who are supervising or helping in all the numerous activities. Although playgroup organizing and supervising can be undertaken on a voluntary basis, high standards and a responsible approach must be maintained if playgroups are successfully to fill the everwidening gap between supply and demand for preschool play education.

EQUIPMENT

Provision. Activities for one or two children need to be just as numerous and varied as for a large number and this basic truth favors the larger group. Once screens, toys, sand, water, and so on have been provided, they might as well be used to full capacity by a larger number of children on the grounds that they don't all want to play with the same thing at the same time. The most economic units to cater for are four—mainly because small tables take four children. This number is just right for affording social contact without bewildering or distracting smaller children. The experience of wider groups can be supplied by intergroup activities or in imaginative games which develop informally. If more than four children wish to play at one game or activity, numbers can be limited by restricting aprons or chairs. It should not be too unbearable to have to wait to play if there is plenty of other material to use in the meantime.

It may not be possible on grounds of lack of capital or space to supply every type of toy from every category at all times but at least one item from each of the following groups should be put out each day.

Water play:	pouring, doll bathing, clothes washing, boat sailing, bubble blowing, paddling
Plastic play:	clay, dough, modeling clay, pastry, mud
Sand:	wet and dry if possible
Painting:	brush painting, finger painting, blob painting, pattern making
Coloring and drawing:	crayons, chalks, colored sticky paper
Family play:	dolls, cots, carriages
Dressing up	
Imaginative play:	playhouse, store, theater, hospital, etc.
Blocks	
Manipulative play:	beads, peg boards, lacing cards, coarse sewing, cutting out, pasting, puzzles
Matching sets:	color, shape, and number sets, Fuzzy Felts, jigsaws
Creative play:	junk, construction sets
Play boards:	farmyards, transportation sets, traffic play board, toy forts, garages
Book corner	
Push and pull toys:	trucks, engines, etc.
Wood play:	hammer play, carpenter's tools

Adventure toys: seesaw, slide, rockers, swing, climb-
                          ing, balancing, and crawling appara-
                          tus
Musical activity: making, listening to, or using music
Story reading and telling

If there is not room for all this material at any one time it may
be necessary to alternate activities or have one type before the
milk break and one afterward, but this is a pity. Free play should
mean a wide choice, not merely freedom to choose from a limited
field.

Care. Neglected, broken, or lost equipment may lead to a narrow choice. Broken items must be mended or replaced and missing pieces must be found as soon as possible. Puzzles scattered in
four corners of the room or doll's bedding in the sandpit are no
use to anyone and the adult in charge must strike a happy
medium between inhibiting play and allowing silly play which
leads to this state. If children feel the urge to destroy or work off
energy, their attention can be guided to other material which
will fulfill this need without spoiling toys that others may wish to
use.

Improvised material is often less serviceable than bought or
specially made equipment and will need replacing more often.
All equipment should be kept in good condition by frequent
cleaning and reasonable handling. Children can be trained to
look after toys but only by example. If they come to the playroom at the beginning of the session and find everything neat
and tidy they have some kind of yardstick to apply. If, on the
other hand, they always have to scrabble at the bottom of the toy
box for enough blocks to build a tower or find pastry rollers
permanently encrusted with dried dough, it will not occur to
them to keep things clean and tidy.

Arrangement. The way in which equipment is arranged is most
important. Those activities needing close supervision and help,
e.g. hammer play, cutting and pasting, pastry or clay, should be
placed so that they can be supervised by one person. If there are
two rooms in use it should be possible to see what is going on at

these tables or units from a door or window. Play such as book corners, jigsaw tables, manipulative play tables can be put together to make a quiet corner. Blocks need a corner which is quiet and away from traffic lanes as does water play. Adventure play needs space away from quiet activities so that movement and reasonable noise is not too distracting for others.

A bare large room with a view of too many activities at once is bewildering for a small child. Good use of playhouse screens or easels or a book corner will break up the space visually so that the playroom becomes a series of smaller spaces each containing a different type of play. If two rooms are available one can be used for noisy games and the other for quiet play. A happy balance between a cluttered, movement-inhibiting arrangement and a clinical lining up of toys should be achieved. One word of warning. It is difficult to persuade children to accept a different arrangement after even a short trial period so thought should be spent on a suitable layout before the children play in it.

Careful storage as described in Chapter 2 can save a great deal of time and effort during setting-out and clearing-up operations.

THE ROLE OF THE ADULT

However pleasant the premises and however good the equipment, the heart of a playgroup is undoubtedly the supervisor. She is responsible for setting the relaxed but creative atmosphere in which children can develop socially, gain knowledge, skill, and self-confidence, and solve emotional problems satisfactorily.

Liking and enjoying small children, having a suitable manner, endless patience, and good health are so obviously necessary that they can be regarded as essentials rather than qualifications for this kind of work. Playgroup supervisors must be emotionally mature women who

understand the value of play;
know how to provide for it;
are practical enough to plan and make equipment if necessary;
are prepared for the noise and seeming untidiness of a group
   of three- to five-year-olds;

can create and maintain a good relationship with the mothers;

are able to organize sessions so that helpers enjoy their work without necessary chores being neglected;

are able and willing to arrive early and leave late so that equipment is ready when children arrive and available until they leave;

are physically strong enough to cope with unpacking and packing equipment for every session;

are prepared to accept too little money for too much work and responsibility;

and, most important of all, realize that they are there merely to serve the children's play needs and should not desire or expect to be a mother substitute.

The successful supervisor or adult helper will automatically sit where she can keep an unobtrusive eye on a number of activities, will know when to offer a suggestion to give life to a flagging interest, will not feel compelled to impress her own personality on children by entertaining them instead of letting them develop their own interests and abilities, will know when to interfere in a fight or help a child out of a difficult situation without his losing face, will have a feeling for equipment and willingly tidy up an activity between groups so that newcomers find it fresh and inviting. Above all she must be willing to learn, read, discuss, and experiment. One educational psychologist summed up all this very well when he likened the role of the adult in successful play experience to that of a good waiter who anticipates and provides for needs, offers suggestions when necessary, and never attempts to direct or force the person he serves.

THE PROBLEMS OF ADAPTING AND USING A BUILDING MEANT FOR ADULTS

Only specialized buildings such as nursery or play schools make provision for small children. In ordinary buildings small tables and chairs can be provided but the large lavatory equipment and high coat pegs are usually irreplaceable fixtures. Some improvisation is necessary to make them comfortable for the three- to five-year age range. Stools or boxes to stand on in lavatories, washbowls placed on chairs or on a low shelf with a jug of water and a bucket for pouring away—all help to encourage small children to be independent. Heavy swing doors into cloakrooms should be safely propped open with a pile of chairs or a large weight.

Individual towels and washcloths should be hung near the washbasins. A special batten fitted with named hooks can be fixed to a wall or suspended by rope loops from suitable hooks in a wall. The towels must not be hung so close together that they overlap or the advantages of separate towels is lost. Paper towels are favored by some authorities but they are not very pleasant or easy to manage. If they are used, a receptacle which allows used towels to be put in but not taken out should be provided. A covered plastic bucket which has a small hole cut in the lid would do. A similar or smaller receptacle for used paper handkerchiefs should be put in some suitable position so that children can reach it for themselves.

A clothespin can be used to keep shoes and boots in pairs if lockers are out of the question. A doweling rod supported at each end by a chair or special stand could be used to hold coats on coathangers. It is worth taking trouble over these domestic details as children soon learn to help themselves if everything is kept within their reach.

HYGIENE

A high standard of cleanliness is essential for a playgroup. Dirty, dusty, gloomy premises are depressing for children just as for adults. Every attempt should be made to avoid cross-infection although most children contract the childish diseases when they come into contact with a number of children, whether their first experience of a group is before five or after five. Normal school rules about how long to exclude children after having the various diseases and ailments should be followed. The experienced supervisor can tell when a child does not look his normal self and should ask the mother to keep him at home for a while.

Cleaning cloths and tea-towels must be kept scrupulously clean. A double set is useful as this allows one set in use and one set drying for each day. Glasses should be kept upturned on a clean tray and covered with a clean cloth. It is tempting to stack plastic glasses inside each other if space is short but this should be avoided. Soaking regularly in a weak antiseptic solution is a good plan. These rules need not become a fad or inhibit satisfactory play, but the precautions necessary for large numbers are always more stringent than those for individual or family units.

A good playgroup is an exciting, rewarding place. A bad one is worse than the most restricted home.

15

The Ultimate Goal

ALL AUTHORITIES on child welfare and sociology agree on the need for a rich environment and wide experience in the pre-school years. It is the relative importance of this aspect of education which is in doubt when financial allocations are discussed. The general lack of money spent in Great Britain on implementing the recommendations of the 1944 Education Act has meant not enough provision for all age groups at all levels. Most parents, having to consider the needs of their child from birth to ultimate fulfillment as an adult, would probably opt for more university places than nursery schools given the choice. But must it be a choice? It is our generation which must decide whether our living conditions, while improving materially, are becoming stultifying for our children. Infants possess when born all that is necessary to enable them to grow, learn, develop. We can allow this process to take its natural course or we can inadvertently inhibit it. The rise in delinquency figures alone would indicate that we are going sadly awry somewhere.

Amateur playgroups are a temporary answer. Perhaps their greatest value lies in providing another dimension of preschool experience to be considered along with the advantages and disadvantages of the present State provision. They are economical in that they fit in with other activities and so can share buildings if adequate regard is paid to their special needs. Costs are cut to a minimum if voluntary help is obtained in the fields of administration and provision of equipment. They provide a close link with home and are a source of information, help, and ideas for parents so that the children's lives are improved at home as well as by the time they spend at the playgroup. Some kind of compromise might include the good features of each type of preschool establishment to the gain of the community and relief of the Exchequer.

In the meantime architects and town planners must be bludgeoned into awareness of long-term social needs. The people who hold the pursestrings must prepare themselves to do more than pay perfunctory lip service to the generation which they will require to support them in their old age. Hospital authorities must pursue their new studies on the factors which accelerate and inhibit the progress made by sick children, and consider carefully whether they do all that could be done to maintain the right atmosphere and provide the right material for play.

Those trustees and management committees in charge of community rooms and halls should accept that the relative profitability of renting to playgroups or for Bingo sessions must be measured in terms of social benefit as well as financial gain. Authorities concerned with training teachers should include training for playgroup work in existing courses and institute special courses for mature women who wish to start a career in this new field. Members of councils must realize that their power and influence can help or hinder a great deal and should consider the matter sociologically rather than in the light of their own personal experience with children. Parents must regard adequate play space as being as inevitable as baby carriage space, and realize that companionship is as necessary as fresh air, and play material as important as food.

We want our children to grow up accepting and being able to live within their environment without letting it conquer them, with the ability to communicate with and respect their fellow beings without losing their individuality, with the imagination to dream dreams and the courage to go out into the world and make them come true.

And where does providing play material come among all these lofty hopes and ideals? As I said at the beginning, it is a good first step we can all take.

Appendix A

Reprinted by arrangement with Bureau of Child Development and Parent Education, University of the State of New York.

A FEW SUGGESTED BOOKS FOR CHILDREN
THREE TO FIVE

Adelson, Leone. *Please Pass the Grass!* McKay. 1960. $3.75.

*Beim, Lorraine and Jerrold. *Two Is a Team.* Harcourt. 1945. $2.75.

Birnbaum, A. *Green Eyes.* Golden Press. 1953. $3.95.

*Brenner, Barbara and Katzoff, Sy. *Barto Takes the Subway.* Viking. 1961. $2.50.

*Brown, J. P. *Ronnie's Wish.* Friendship. 1954. $1.50.

Brown, Marcia. *The Little Carousel.* Scribner. 1946. $2.95.

Brown, M. W. *Goodnight, Moon.* Harper. 1947. $2.95.

————. *The Important Book.* Harper. 1949. $3.

————. *The Little Fur Family.* Harper. 1951. $2.75.

————. *The Summer Noisy Book.* Harper. 1951. $2.95.

————. *Where Have You Been?* Hastings. 1963. $2.25.

Buckley, H. E. *Grandfather and I.* Lothrop. 1959. $2.75.

We suggest that there is no substitute for firsthand inspection of books before purchasing them. With the help of a good book list it is a wise policy then to browse through children's books in libraries or bookshops before making final selections.

The bibliography includes many outstanding authors who have written a number of fine books for young children. On the list you will find only a few representative examples of their work. For your collection it is likely that you will wish to add other titles by these writers.

* Indicates books which introduce interracial or intercultural concepts in text or pictures. Since such books today are of particular interest, we have included a larger number of them than might ordinarily appear in a well-balanced bibliography. (A few make such a contribution through their pictures that we have placed them on the list even though the text is more suited to older children.)

————. *Josie and the Snow.* Lothrop. 1964. $2.95.

Burton, V. L. *Katy and the Big Snow.* Houghton. 1943. $3.25.

Child Study Association of America. *Read to Me Again.* Crowell. 1961. $2.95.

Daly, Kathleen. *The Cat Book.* Golden Press. 1964. $1. (Golden-craft Binding $2.65).

De Regniers, B. S. *Who Likes the Sun?* Harcourt. 1961. $3.

Dorian, Marguerite. *When the Snow Is Blue.* Lothrop. 1959. $2.75.

Downer, M. L. *The Flower.* W. R. Scott. 1959. $2.50.

Du Bois, W. P. *Bear Party.* Viking. 1963. $3.

Einsel, Walter. *Did You Ever See?* W. R. Scott. 1962. $3.

Emberley, Barbara and Ed. *Night's Nice.* Doubleday. 1963. $1.95.

*Ets, M. H. *Gilberto and the Wind.* Viking. 1963. $3.

————. *Play with Me.* Viking. 1955. $2.75.

Flack, Marjorie. *Angus and the Ducks.* Doubleday. 1939. $2.25.

————. *Ask Mr. Bear.* McMillan. rev. 1932. $2.

Françoise. *Jeanne-Marie Counts Her Sheep.* Scribner. 1957. $2.95.

Gag, Wanda. *Millions of Cats.* Coward. 1928. $2.50.

Geismer, B. P. and Suter, A. B. *Very Young Verses.* Houghton. 1945. $3.

Green, M. M. *Everybody Eats.* W. R. Scott. 1961. $2.

Ipcar, Dahlov. *Wild and Tame Animals.* Doubleday. 1963. $2.75.

Jacobs, L. B. *Just Around the Corner.* Holt. 1964. $3.50.

*Keats, E. J. *The Snowy Day.* Viking. 1962. $3.

*————. *Whistle for Willie.* Viking. 1964. $3.50.

Kessler, and Leonard, Ethel. *All Aboard the Train.* Doubleday. 1964. $2.95.

————. *Do Baby Bears Sit in Chairs?* Doubleday. 1961. $2.50.

————. *Kim and Me.* Doubleday. 1960. $2.

Krauss, Ruth. *The Backward Day.* Harper. 1950. $2.95.

————. *The Bundle Book.* Harper. 1951. $3.

————. *The Growing Story.* Harper. 1947. $3.25.

Lenski, Lois. *Davy Goes Places.* Walck. 1961. $1.95.

————. *I Like Winter.* Walck. 1950. $1.95.

————. *Let's Play House.* Walck. 1944. $2.25.

McGovern, Ann. *Who Has a Secret?* Houghton. 1964. $3.25.

*Marino, Dorothy. *Where Are the Mothers?* Lippincott. 1959. $2.50.

Miles, Betty. *A House for Everyone.* Knopf. 1958. $3.25.

Minarik, E. H. *Little Bear.* Harper. 1957. $1.95.

Munari, Bruno. *Zoo.* World. Pub. 1963. $3.50.

Petersham, Maud and Miska. *The Box with Red Wheels.* Macmillan. 1949. $2.95.

Puner, H. W. *Daddies—What They Do All Day.* Lothrop. 1956. $2.95.

Rice, Inez. *A Long Long Time.* Lothrop. 1964. $3.50.

Risom, Ole. *I Am a Mouse.* Golden Press. 1964. $1. (Goldencraft Binding $2.65).

Rojanovsky, Feodor, illus. *The Tall Book of Mother Goose.* Harper. 1942. $1.95.

Rothschild, Alice. *Fruit Is Ripe for Timothy.* W. R. Scott. 1963. $3.25.

Schick, Eleanor. *A Surprise in the Forest.* Harper. 1964. $1.95.

Schlein, Miriam. *Snow Time.* Whitman. 1962. $2.75.

Schneider, Nina. *While Susie Sleeps.* W. R. Scott. 1959. $3.

Selsam, Millicent. *Seeds and More Seeds.* Harper. 1959. $1.95.

*Shackelford, J. D. *My Happy Days.* Associated Pub. 1944. $2.65.

*Simon, Norma. *Hanukkah in My House.* United Synagogue Commission on Jewish Education. 1960. 95¢.

Skaar, Grace. *The Little Red House.* W. R. Scott. 1955. $2.25.

———. *Nothing but Cats, Cats, Cats.* W. R. Scott. 1947. $2.

Slobodkina, Esphyr. *Caps for Sale.* W. R. Scott. 1947. $2.75.

*Tooze, Ruth. *Our Rice Village in Cambodia.* Viking. 1963. $2.75.

Tresselt, Alvin. *Rain Drop Splash.* Lothrop. 1946. $2.95.

———. *Wake up, City!* Lothrop. 1957. $2.95.

Tudor, Tasha. *A Is for Annabelle.* Walck. 1954. $3.25.

———. *Samantha's Surprise.* Lippincott. 1964. $2.75.

Udry, J. M. *A Tree is Nice.* Harper. 1956. $2.75.

Ungerer, Tomi. *Snail, Where Are You?* Harper. 1962. $2.50.

*Williamson, Stan. *The No-Bark Dog.* Follett. 1962. $1.

Wright, Ethel. *Saturday Walk.* W. R. Scott. 1954. $2.50.

*Yashima, Taro. *Umbrella.* Viking. 1958. $3.

Ylla and Gregor, Arthur. *Animal Babies.* Harper. 1959. $3.50.

Zaffo, G. J. *Giant Nursery Book of Things that Go.* Doubleday. 1959. $3.95.

Zion, Gene. *Harry the Dirty Dog.* Harper. 1956. $3.25.

———. *Really Spring.* Harper. 1956. $3.50.

Zolotow, Charlotte. *The Poodle Who Barked at the Wind.* Lothrop. 1964. $2.95.

———. *The Sleepy Book.* Lothrop. 1958. $2.95.

The following sources may also be helpful in choosing books for the preschool child:

Bibliography of Books for Children. 1962 Bulletin 37. $1.50.
   Association for Childhood Education International, 3615 Wisconsin Avenue, N.W., Washington, D.C. 20016.

Children's Catalog. 10th ed. rev. 1961. $12.
    H. W. Wilson Co. (Available in school and public libraries.)
The Horn Book Magazine. Published six times a year. $5 annually.
    Horn Book, Inc., 585 Boylston Street, Boston, Mass. 02116.
School Library Journal. Issued the 15th of the month, September
    through May. $5 annually.
    R. R. Bowker Co., 1180 Avenue of the Americas, New York, N.Y.
    10036 (Usually available in school and public libraries.)

A FEW SUGGESTED BOOKS FOR CHILDREN
FIVE TO SIX

*Ames, Jocelyn and Lee. *City Street Games.* Holt. 1963. $1.95.
Beim, Jerrold. *Sir Halloween.* Morrow. 1959. $2.75.
Bemelmans, Ludwig. *Madeline.* Viking. 1939. $3.50.
Benedick, Jeanne. *A Fresh Look at Night.* Watts. 1963. $2.65.
Bethel, Jean. *The Monkey in the Rocket.* Grosset. 1962. 59¢.
Blough, G. O. *Soon after September: The Story of Living Things in
    Winter.* McGraw. 1960. $2.75.
*Bonsall, C. N. *The Case of the Hungry Stranger.* Harper. 1963. $1.95.
Borten, Helen, *Do You Hear What I Hear?* Abelard. 1960. $2.75.
Brown, Marcia. *Once a Mouse.* Scribner. 1961. $3.25.
Brown, M. W. *The Golden Egg Book.* Golden Press. 1947. $1.99.
———. *Nibble, Nibble.* W. R Scott. 1959. $3.75.
———. *Wait till the Moon is Full.* Harper. 1948. $2.95.
Buell, E. L., ed. *A Treasury of Little Golden Books.* Golden Press.
    1960. $3.95.
Burchard, Peter. *The Carol Moran.* Macmillan. 1958. $3.50.
Burton, V. L. *Mike Mulligan and His Steam Shovel.* Hougton. 1939.
    $3.25.
Cameron, Polly. *I Can't, Said the Ant: A Second Book of Nonsense.*
    Coward. 1961. $2.50.
*Chanover, Hyman and Alice. *Happy Hanukkah, Everybody.* United
    Synagogue Commission on Jewish Education. 1954. $1.25.
Child Study Association of America. *Read-to-Me Storybook.* Crowell.
    1947. $2.95.
Collier, Ethel. *The Birthday Tree.* W. R. Scott. 1961. $3.25.
Conklin, G. P. *We Like Bugs.* Holiday. 1962. $3.25.
De Regniers, B. S. *The Shadow Book.* Harcourt. 1960. $2.75.
———. *The Snow Party.* Pantheon. 1959. $2.75.
———. *Something Special.* Harcourt. 1958. $2.50.
Du Bois, W. P. *Otto in Africa.* Viking. 1961. $2.50.

Everson, Dale. *Mrs. Popover Goes to the Zoo.* Morrow. 1963. $2.95.

Fatio, Louise. *The Happy Lion and the Bear.* McGraw. 1964. $2.95.

*Felt, Sue. *Rosa-Too-Little.* Doubleday. 1950. $2.50.

Fisher, Aileen. *Cricket in a Thicket.* Scribner. 1963. $2.95.

———. *Going Barefoot.* Crowell. 1960. $3.50.

Flack, Marjorie. *Boats on the River.* Viking. 1946. $3.50.

———. *The Story About Ping.* Viking. 1933. $1.75.

———. *Tim Tadpole and the Great Bullfrog.* Doubleday. 1959. $2.50.

Floethe, L. L. *The Cowboy on the Ranch.* Scribner. 1959. $3.25.

Françoise. *What Time Is It, Jeanne-Marie?* Scribner. 1963. $3.25.

Freeman, Don. *Come Again, Pelican.* Viking. 1961. $3.

Gag, Wanda. *Gone Is Gone.* Coward. 1935. $2.

Goudey, A. E. *Butterfly Time.* Scribner. 1964. $3.25.

———. *The Day We Saw the Sun Come Up.* Scribner. 1961. $3.25.

Green, M. M. *Is It Hard? Is It Easy?* W. R. Scott. 1960. $3.

*Hader, Berta and Elmer. *Snow in the City.* Macmillan. 1963. $3.50.

*Holding, James. *The Lazy Little Zulu.* Morrow. 1962. $3.25.

*———. *Mr. Moonlight and Omar.* Morrow. 1963. $3.25.

Hurd, E. T. and Clement. *Mr. Charlie's Gas Station.* Lippincott. 1956. $2.75.

Ipcar, Dahlov. *Ten Big Farms.* Knopf. 1958. $2.50.

Joslin, Sesyle. *What Do You Say, Dear?* W. R. Scott. 1958. $2.75.

*Katzoff, Betty. *Cathy's First School.* Knopf. 1964. $2.95.

*Keats, E. J. and Cherr, Pat. *My Dog Is Lost.* Crowell. 1960. $2.95.

Krauss, Ruth. *The Big World and the Little House.* Harper. 1956. $3.25.

*Lansdown, Brenda. *Galumph!* Houghton. 1963. $3.

Lenski, Lois. *Policeman Small.* Walck. 1962. $2.25.

Lewis, Claudia. *When I Go to the Moon.* Macmillan. 1961. $3.

*Lexau, J. M. *Benjie.* Dial. 1964. $3.

*———. *Maria.* Dial. 1964. $2.95.

Liang, Yen. *The Skyscraper.* Lippincott. 1958. $3.50.

McCloskey, Robert. *Make Way for Ducklings.* Viking. 1941. $3.50.

McGovern, Ann. *Zoo, Where Are You?* Harper. 1964. $3.50.

Marino, Dorothy. *Buzzy Bear in the Garden.* Watts. 1963. $2.95.

*Martin, P. M. *No, No, Rosina.* Putnam. 1964. $2.75.

Meeks, E. M. *Jeff and Mr. James' Pond.* Lothrop. 1962. $2.95.

Merrill, Jean. *Tell About the Cowbarn, Daddy.* W. R. Scott. 1963. $3.50.

Miles, Betty. *A Day of Summer.* Knopf. 1960. $2.75.

———. *Mr. Turtle's Mystery.* Knopf. 1961. $2.75.

Miller, Edna. *Mousekin's Golden House.* Prentice-Hall. 1964. $3.50.

Mitchell, L. S. and Black, I. S., ed. *Believe and Make-Believe.* Dutton. 1956. $3.95.

*Ness, Evaline. *Josefina February.* Scribner. 1963. $3.25.

*Politi, Leo. *Moy Moy.* Scribner. 1960. $3.25.

*———. *Rosa.* Scribner. 1963. $3.25.

*Ormsby, V. H. *The Big Banyan Tree.* Lippincott. 1964. $2.95.

*———. *Twenty-One Children.* Lippincott. 1957. $2.25.

*Randall, B. E. *Fun for Chris.* Whitman. 1956. $1.75.

Rey, H. A. *Curious George.* Houghton. 1941. $3.25.

———. *Curious George Learns the Alphabet.* Houghton. 1963. $3.25.

Russell, S. P. *All Kinds of Legs.* Bobbs. 1963. $2.75.

Schlein, Miriam. *Heavy Is a Hippopotamus.* W. R. Scott. 1954. $2.75.

———. *The Pile of Junk.* Abelard. 1962. $2.75.

Schwartz, Julius. *The Earth Is Your Space Ship.* McGraw. 1963. $2.50.

———. *I Know a Magic House.* McGraw. 1956. $2.75.

Selsam, Millicent. *A Time for Sleep: How Animals Rest.* W. R. Scott. 1953. $2.75.

———. *You and the World Around You.* Doubleday. 1963. $3.50.

Seuss, Dr. *And to Think that I Saw It on Mulberry Street.* Vanguard. 1937. $2.95.

———. *Dr. Seuss' ABC.* Random. 1963. $1.95.

*Sharpe, S. G. *Tobe.* University of North Carolina Press. 1939. $2.75.

*Showers, Paul. *Look at Your Eyes.* Crowell. 1962. $2.75.

Simon, Mona and Howard. *If You Were an Eel, How Would You Feel?* Follett. 1963. $2.95.

Stevenson, R. L. *A Child's Garden of Verses.* Golden Press. 1951. $1.95.

*Sutherland, Efua. *Playtime in Africa.* Atheneum. 1962. $3.

*Tarry, Ellen, and Ets, M. H. *My Dog Rinty.* Viking. 1946. $3.

Thayer, Jane. *Andy and the Runaway Horse.* Morrow. 1963. $2.75.

Tresselt, Alvin. *Autumn Harvest.* Lothrop. 1951. $2.95.

———. *The Mitten.* Lothrop. 1964. $2.95.

———. *White Snow, Bright Snow.* Lothrop. 1947. $2.95.

*Uchida, Yoshiko. *Sumi's Prize.* Scribner. 1964. $3.25.

Warburg, S. S. *My Very Own Special, Particular, Private and Personal Cat.* Houghton. 1963. $3.25.

Webber, Irma. *Travelers All.* W. R. Scott. 1944. $2.50.

———. *Up Above and Down Below.* W. R. Scott. 1943. $2.50.

Zaffo, George. *The Big Book of Real Trucks.* Grosset. 1950. $1.

Zion, Gene. *The Plant Sitter.* Harper. 1959. $3.25.

Zolotow, Charlotte. *The Sky Was Blue.* Harper. 1963. $2.95.

———. *The Storm Book.* Harper. 1952. $2.95.

Appendix B

1. Association for Childhood Education International
   3615 Wisconsin Ave., N.W.
   Washington, D.C. 20016

2. Bank Street College of Education
   69 Bank Street
   New York City, 10014

3. Child Study Association of America, Inc.
   9 East 89th Street
   New York City, 10028

4. National Association for Education of Young Children
   3700 Massachusetts Avenue, N.W.
   Washington, D.C. 20016

SOURCES FOR EQUIPMENT AND SUPPLIES

1. Childplay
   43 E. 19th Street
   New York City, 10003

2. Childcraft
   155 East 23rd Street
   New York City, 10010

3. Community Playthings
   Rifton, New York 12471

4. Creative Playthings, Inc.
   Order Dept.: P.O. Box 1100
   Princeton, New Jersey

Sales Office: 1 Rockefeller Center
New York City, 10020

5. Novo Education Toy & Equipment Co.
585 6th Avenue
New York City, 10011

6. Musicon Inc.
42–00 Vernon Blvd.
Long Island City
N.Y. 11101

Catalogs may be obtained by writing to these companies. Most of these companies carry extensive lines of equipment and supplies both for outdoor as well as indoor play. Child size furniture suitable for home or playgroups is also available.

*Some other Penguin books
are described on the
following pages*

PELICAN ORIGINAL
A814

ORIGINS AND GROWTH OF
MODERN EDUCATION

Elizabeth S. Lawrence. A summary of educational thought from ancient times to the present day, which shows that many tenets of modern education have in fact been recurring themes in educational philosophy throughout the ages. Quotes from the Greeks and Romans, from the Renaissance, from the seventeenth century, from Rousseau, Pestalozzi, Froebel, and Montessori, reveal certain basic ideas being reiterated again and again: education is a drawing out, not a putting in; the object of education is the development of the whole man, not merely of the intellect; the importance of books and knowledge can be exaggerated; in the right climate the child will learn as naturally as a plant grows. The book makes clear that much of what is considered revolutionary in education today has its roots deep in the past.

PUFFIN BOOKS

Editor: Kaye Webb

PS200

THE PUFFIN BOOK OF
NURSERY RHYMES

For centuries each generation has been linked to the next by the shared laughter of nursery rhymes; and it has been said that one of the best investments a family can make is a good nursery rhyme book.

Here is a notable collection of nursery rhymes, for it is a fresh gathering from the memories of grandmothers and the byways of folk literature. As well as containing all the familiar jingles it introduces a number of traditional rhymes which have hitherto been known only locally or in individual families. In fact, this is a sparkling treasury of memorable verses, as lovingly planned as a poetry anthology, annotated and indexed both by subject and by first lines. To complete the pleasure, the book is illustrated on almost every page with exquisite pictures by Pauline Baynes.

This is the first comprehensive collection of nursery rhymes to be produced as a paperback, and it has been specially prepared by two of the foremost authorities on children's lore.

PUFFIN BOOKS
Editor: Kaye Webb
PS 237

Something To Do

Here at last is a book to fill up all the wet days and dull days that produce the question 'What can I do?' in every family. *Something To Do* has suggestions for things children can do at home, indoors and outside, without spending much money or being a terrible nuisance.

Each month has a separate chapter so that the games and ideas will fit in with the proper season. February, for instance, that month of sniffles and chicken pox and measles, has a special section of Things To Do in Bed, and August, the holiday month, has a bunch of ideas to pass the time while travelling. Every month has its own special flower and bird to look for. There are tempting dishes to cook, things to make, games to play, and instructions for keeping pets.

This is every busy mother's *vade mecum*. It will refresh her memory on half-forgotten pastimes, and save her any amount of brain-searching with its detailed information and plans for practical entertainments.